THE EVERYTHING

Knots Book

Dear Reader:

I was always intrigued by how much we use rope and string in our daily lives and yet know so little about knotting them. Until I took up knot tying as a hobby, I knew what most people know about knotting; I knew how to tie my shoes, tie a necktie, and fasten a rope to an object without it looking too much like a rat's nest.

I always told myself that I would get a knot book someday and learn to tie properly, but passed up on some opportunities, partly because I was intimidated at the thought of following the diagrams and trying to remember the crossings. When I finally sat down and spent some time to learn knotting, I discovered that there is an art and orderliness to it that I never would have imagined. It is my intention that this book will bring this same realization to you and you will enjoy learning the art of knot tying as much as I have enjoyed teaching it to you.

Randy Penn

THE

EVERYTHING®
Series

The handy, accessible books in this series give you all you need to tackle a difficult project, gain a new hobby, or even brush up on something you learned back in school but have since forgotten. You can read cover to cover or just pick out information from the four useful boxes.

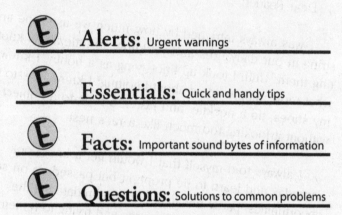

Alerts: Urgent warnings

Essentials: Quick and handy tips

Facts: Important sound bytes of information

Questions: Solutions to common problems

When you're done reading, you can finally
say you know EVERYTHING®!

EDITORIAL

Publisher: Karen Cooper
Director of Acquisitions and Innovation: Paula Munier
Managing Editor, Everything® Series: Lisa Laing
Copy Chief: Casey Ebert
Assistant Production Editor: Jacob Erickson
Acquisitions Editor: Kate Powers
Senior Development Editor: Brett Palana-Shanahan
Associate Development Editor: Hillary Thompson
Editorial Assistant: Ross Weisman
Everything® Series Cover Designer: Erin Alexander
Layout Designers: Colleen Cunningham,
Elisabeth Lariviere, Denise Wallace

Visit the entire Everything® series at www.everything.com

THE
EVERYTHING®
KNOTS
BOOK

Step-by-step instructions for tying any knot

Randy Penn

Adams Media
New York London Toronto Sydney New Delhi

Adams Media
An Imprint of Simon & Schuster, Inc.
57 Littlefield Street
Avon, Massachusetts 02322

An Everything® Series Book.
Everything® and everything.com® are registered trademarks of Simon & Schuster, Inc.

ADAMS MEDIA and colophon are trademarks of Simon and Schuster.

For information about special discounts for bulk purchases, please contact Simon & Schuster Special Sales at 1-866-506-1949 or business@simonandschuster.com.

The Simon & Schuster Speakers Bureau can bring authors to your live event. For more information or to book an event contact the Simon & Schuster Speakers Bureau at 1-866-248-3049 or visit our website at www.simonspeakers.com.

Manufactured in the United States of America

20 19

Library of Congress Cataloging-in-Publication Data has been applied for.

ISBN 978-1-59337-032-9

Contents

Top Ten Reasons
for Learning Knots

1. Knotting will help you in endeavors you already enjoy. If you're an avid camper, you'll find setting up camp a lot easier once you have knotting skills.

2. It will also help you get involved in new activities. If you've never tried boating, learning knots will take you a step closer to this activity.

3. Knotting is a useful skill in many crafts.

4. Tying cordage properly will make you look competent.

5. You will be able to manage ropes of different sizes and materials.

6. You will learn how to tie safer knots that won't untie under duress.

7. You'll react better if you need to tie a knot in an emergency.

8. You'll find more uses for rope, like securing cargo to your bicycle or motorcycle.

9. You'll be able to rely on cordage to make a variety of repairs.

10. Most importantly, you'll learn how to do the job right.

Acknowledgments

I would like to give my sincere thanks and appreciation to the many members of the International Guild of Knot Tyers who have shared their knowledge with me over the years. Through many branches around the world, they continue to provide knowledge and education to all those who ask. Their membership is open to all who are interested in sharing their knowledge and learning from others.

I would also like to thank Patricia Kurtz, who has been an enormous help throughout this project. It couldn't have been easy reading my first drafts of knotting instructions, and her patience is greatly appreciated.

Introduction

KNOT TYING IS A PURSUIT that can change from intimidating to entertaining with just a little effort. This book is designed to make that effort both enjoyable and educational. To learn about knotting is to learn how humankind fashioned a handhold on its environment since before recorded history and how this remains important today as new types of ropes are created and people continue to experiment with the best knots to tame them with.

This book features knots and related skills that will have you taming your environment to suit your needs—be they for practical applications or just for fun. There are no specific reference lists here telling you which knots you should use for camping and which you should use for sailing, for example. Instead, you will have the opportunity to learn the basic concepts of using knots as tools, leading you chapter by chapter through various types of knots. If this book were about hand tools, it would not emphasize which tools to use on a car and which to use on a washing machine, but would teach the basic principles behind their use. It might cover how to tell when a wrench or spanner might be better to use than pliers, and vice versa. There would also be advice on how to make do with another tool that may not be meant for the job. Knowledge like this would enable you to make your own choice about what tool to use in a variety of circumstances.

Knots are the tools for using rope. With a little practice and experience with knots, a piece of rope becomes much more than just a line—it becomes the equivalent of an entire toolbox of possibilities.

The chapters on knots are categorized by function. They include stopper knots for the ends of rope, knots for joining ropes together, making loops, fastening ropes to objects, binding objects, knots for decoration, and knots for specific activities. Additional chapters cover subjects that both complement and directly assist you in acquiring, sharing, and using the knowledge of knot tying. In this manner, acquiring the knowledge of knots should not be done as a standalone activity. Additional information is provided here to allow the experience of knotting to encompass much more than just knowing twists and turns.

Basic properties of knots are dependent on the rope you use. Ropes vary widely, so their properties figure into how they are chosen for specific uses and also affect which knots work best for them. The information contained here will help you choose the best ropes for your needs and teach you how to knot them effectively.

Learning to tie knots can be considered a skill in itself, so much information and many tips are provided to help you. If you have encountered stumbling blocks in the past when trying to learn knots, you will find helpful hints to overcome them.

Plus, there's information on the history of knots, tips on how to teach knot-tying techniques to others, and additional resource listings to help you expand your exploration of knots beyond this book.

The knots in this book were chosen based on popular convention, historical significance, and use of common structures shared with other knots. In tying these knots you will be both following in the steps of history and taking part in the ever-increasing body of knowledge available to the modern knot tyer. It is hard to express in words the joy and confidence that a young child feels from learning a knot. There is something about knots that creates the feeling of being able to function in the world and provides a sense of confidence in your own abilities.

A Little History and Perspective

IT'S SAID THAT IF YOU LOOK AT WHERE you have been, it helps to see where you are going. Just a small glance at the history of knotting shows that it is an integral part of our past and will continue to be a part of our present and future.

Prehistoric Origins

We don't know much about how knots and cordage were used in times long before recorded history, but we can make some educated guesses based on the scant traces left of early human lives as well as what we know about that environment. Taking into account what materials were at hand and what inspiration was available from the surroundings, many conclusions can be drawn.

Early Cordage Materials

Both plant and animal materials were available to prehistoric humans to be used as cordage. Numerous plants are made of strong fibers that provide structural strength. Some plants—such as vines—can be used as cordage without any preparation at all. Additionally, early hunters had a wide choice of animals as a resource. Throughout more recent history, humans have used many parts of animals for cordage. Hides were cut into thin strips as a ready source of tying materials. Tendons were especially strong. And many other parts of animals have been used throughout the ages. Before recorded history, humans had this same "hardware store" available to them as in more recent times.

Ⓔ QUESTION?

How would a caveman react if he were to come across a roll of modern synthetic twine? Would he marvel at its strength? Probably. Modern synthetics are many times stronger than their equivalent size in natural fibers. Nevertheless, he may not want to use our modern cordage. He might find that the knots he was using to secure his more natural cordage would not hold on the more slippery modern material.

Inspired by Nature

Early humans must have been inspired to tie their first knots by what they saw around them. Spider webs, bird nests, and even the complex structures of many plants may have given them a hint as to how to proceed. Occasionally small game would become tangled in undergrowth, and even fish would become entangled in underwater growth. Nature can be a great teacher of what cordage can accomplish.

Ⓔ FACT

There are many knot tyers in the animal kingdom. Gorillas have been seen tying Granny Knots and even Square Knots to hold saplings down in their nests. Captive monkeys are known to untie and retie knots found in their cages. The hagfish ties itself in an overhand knot, and the weaverbird ties a number of knots in nest making.

Some occurrences in the environment probably helped early knot tyers to improve the use of cordage. Perhaps they noticed that when they pulled some twigs apart, two of them would bind if their ends happened to have been bent and overlapped. Plants sometimes grow in Half Hitches around one another. Overhand Knots seem to form spontaneously in cordlike materials. You have, no doubt, seen knots suddenly appear in garden hoses and electrical cords. So, it is not a stretch to imagine that Overhand Knots, Half Hitches, and various twists in materials could have been tied on purpose in an attempt to duplicate nature.

Historical Evidence

Ancient artifacts tell us a wide-ranging story about our past. This story has its gaps, especially when it comes to the history of knotting. That is not surprising when you consider that the natural materials cordage was made from decays in almost all environments. However, the surviving samples provide direct evidence of early humans incorporating the technology of knotting into how they lived.

Indirect Evidence of Knot Tying

Even when artifacts have no surviving cordage with them, the items can still give us clues that they were used with cordage. For instance, a small decorative jewelry-like item that has a hole cut into it was probably suspended from a cord. Some of the artifacts even show wear at the place where the string would have been tied. Other items have deep indentations that would have needed knotting to hold them in place. Spears and hatchets were shaped to facilitate binding to a shaft. Pottery fragments show indentations of three-strand rope and a surprising variety of decorative knotting. Early artwork in both paintings and carvings also depict knotting.

Direct Evidence of Knot Tying

In more recent times, of course, we have actual pieces of knotting to reveal glimpses of our past. These samples show uses in just about all aspects of life, from decorative objects to hunting-and-gathering instruments. Many cultures have shown ingenuity in making cordage with the materials available; others have truly taken knot tying to an art form.

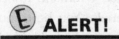 **ALERT!**

Knot making hasn't changed much over the years. Objects tied thousands of years ago were tied much as they would be tied today. Nets were tied with the same mesh knot that would be used today in a hand-tied net.

Signs of Progress

Civilization has come a long way since humans first coaxed fish out of a stream with a woven tangle of vines, but we didn't do it all at once. We accomplished it in many stages, with a steady application of knotting all the way. Whenever humans have learned something new, they have updated the technology of cordage and knotting along with it. For many early users of knots and cordage, being able to tie a line to a fishing hook or lash a spear to a shaft meant being able to feed their family. Being able to make lashings meant building structures to protect the family from the elements. It meant survival. Knot tying was not an optional activity—it was a way of life. Humankind has improved methods for hunting, warring, and surviving the elements, and increased knotting skills went hand in hand with these advances. When it came time to sail the seas, domesticate cattle, and even keep track of numbers and dates, knots continued to be used in new ways.

New cultures, religions, and technologies brought on many changes, and humans learned various new professions. Clothes and blankets take considerable time to tie and weave. When the industrial revolution came along, the first machines made were for tying knots and weaving. Rope had been mass-produced long before then. Through all these changes, few endeavors were taken up without laying in a major supply of cordage.

 FACT

> The majority of early artwork portrayed knots without precise details. In some cases it may have been due to the fact that knots are tricky to draw accurately. Some paintings of large sailing warships in action have large sections of the rigging clouded by cannon smoke, presumably to avoid the labor of rendering all the details.

Beyond Basic Functions

The existence of knots meant more than just function to our ancestors. As early humans learned to apply symbolism, knots played a key role. Even superstitious beliefs became attached to knots, thereby giving them more than just a symbolic role.

A Means of Representation

As humankind's use of symbolism and communication developed, knots took on new meaning by way of representation. As people learned to count days, they counted them with knots on a string.

Did you ever wonder how people kept track of meetings before appointment books and PDAs? For some, a bit of string was all that was needed to keep an appointment. Often an invitation to a meeting consisted of a string with a number of knots tied in it to represent the number of days until the event. They would be untied one per day until time was up.

By far the most elaborate record keeping ever done was on knotted strings, or *quipus*, by the Inca of Peru. Each *quipu* was a system of many strands branching off a central cord. The knots on these strands represented all the data needed to administer an empire, including mathematics, census figures, taxes, crops, herds, and many other things. Using knots allowed the Inca to record and calculate data without having a written language.

(E) ESSENTIAL

Once humans had taken a step toward symbolic representation, a knot was no longer a knot. To this day, people knot a string around their finger or knot the corner of a handkerchief to represent something they want to remember.

Magical Properties

As humans' imagination and beliefs continued to develop, knots were believed to hold an influence over the things they represented. Early sailors tied knots to symbolize binding the wind within them, and untying them was believed to release the wind. Similar beliefs were held for illness, love, friendship, and political unities. Healers attempted to bind someone's illness within knots, and then release it harmlessly elsewhere.

What's in a Name?

The names given to knots provide clues about what they meant to our ancestors. One of the first things you may notice about the names of knots is that some of them refer to professions. From Archer and Bell Ringer to Weaver, knots continue to be called by their name-sakes. This implies that they played a key role in these trades.

An important quirk about knotting nomenclature is that some knots have multiple names, and one name can refer to many different knots. When a knot has many different names, it is an indication that, for whatever reason, that knot was significant enough to warrant such attention. Just as there are many words for *snow* in the Eskimo language, important concepts tend to attract multiple labels. When a certain name refers to many different knots, just the opposite can be the case. It can mean that many different knots were used for what the name stood for. A good example of this is the Fisherman's Knot.

Ⓔ ALERT!

Sometimes just hearing the name of a knot can invoke a sense of drama around its use. The name Highwayman's Hitch may lead you to picture someone quick-releasing his horse after doing something nefarious, and possibly to speculate that there may be a Handcuff Knot or Hangman's Noose in his future.

Today and Tomorrow

What has all this history brought us to? Where is it going to take us? For yourself, the answer can only be found with you. Where do you want to be and where do you want to go? For society, the answer is broad and far ranging.

The State of Knot Tying Today

Today some cordage is made out of new synthetic materials, while some is still made of natural fibers. The more slippery of the synthetic materials have made for more careful knot tying, in order to keep the knots themselves from slipping. A vast number of crafts, professions, and activities have brought many new knots into use, each with its own special application and name. Experimenters come up with new knots every day, and ropes of new and different structures even require that splicing be done differently. Decorative knot tyers continue to astound us with their new creations.

However, basic knot tying remains what it has always been— a way to use cordage to help us interact with and control our environment. This is done now and will continue to be done with basic knots that can be readily learned, yet used and shared for a lifetime.

The Learning Process Continues

We are tempted to laugh at our past beliefs and superstitions about knots. But the inner workings of knots are just as mysterious today as any time in the past. Many texts refer to the workings of friction, or the key importance of a "nip" in the knot (that particular part of the knot that can be thought of as "locking" it). While not incorrect, in reality these serve mostly as learning aids. Knots put under high strain do not necessarily result in damage at their nip. In fact, they tend to break just outside the knot. The reason for this is not fully understood, and even computer models only seem to confirm this, without explaining why. This is really not surprising, since the science of the late twentieth century has taught us that there can be infinite complexities within even the most simple of systems.

Ⓔ QUESTION?

Is the complexity and our lack of understanding about the inner workings of knots a problem?
Not at all, because it is not a barrier to their use. If you tie the right knot for the right application, you have done all you can do! It is no more important to understand the topology of a knot than it is to understand the circuitry of a cell phone.

Many avenues of higher learning keep leading us to further research in knots. The higher mathematics of algebraic structures and topology are only beginning to describe knots. Mathematical progress in classifying knots leads to increased understanding in the mechanics of DNA strands and polymers. It also contributes to the study of higher dimensions and theoretical physics. To be sure, history shall someday lump our current understanding of knots with that of the caveman.

A Personal Perspective

What do you want out of knot tying? One way to tell if you want something is to imagine that you already have it. Simply try to cover the many benefits by highlighting a few specific uses. So, let's suppose that you are well versed in knot tying and can apply a bit of twine or rope to almost any relevant situation.

Consider the Benefits

Let's just name a few of the uses you will have for your new knot-tying knowledge. First of all, congratulations on your tremendous increase in strength, since you now know how to multiply your pulling strength with just a simple Trucker's Hitch. Because this hitch can be tied all the way around something, you can apply a crushing force far beyond the strength you had before you became a knot tyer. Your reach is certainly to be admired, too, especially with your ability to tie both locking and sliding loops in the end of rope.

Do you like to be able to handle emergencies? Thank goodness you are an adept knot tyer. Skill with knots and rope is key to many rescue scenarios, from first aid to evacuations. Do you spend time with children? From simple knots to complex crafts, children the world over enjoy learning about knotting.

Knots as Tools

If you are the type of person who always likes to keep a tool kit in your car or truck, now you should include some cordage, both big and small. A broken hose clamp is not necessarily a problem for someone who has small cordage and knows the Constrictor Knot.

For One and All

As you have learned in this chapter, knot tying has been around for as long as humans have had a use for knots. Taking their cue from the natural world around them, early humans used knots to make their weapons, catch food, build shelters, create decorations and adornments, and even keep records. Knots are no less useful today than they were in ancient times. Modern humans are continuing to find new uses for knots and create new ones. Are you ready to join the ranks of the knot makers?

Ⓔ ALERT!

Your knotting skill can be applied to many new activities you may take up. Whether it's a craft or an outdoor activity such as sailing or fishing, your knotting skills will take you a long way.

All about Ropes and Twine

CORDAGE IS THE GENERAL TERM to describe anything you can use to tie a knot—string or twine (for small knots) and line (for nautical knots). This chapter contains all the information you need to know about cordage big and small.

Basic Structure and Materials

Both the structure of rope and the materials it is made of help determine its knot-making properties, allowing you to choose the right rope for your needs. Almost all cordage is built up from threadlike lengths called fibers. How these are twisted or woven together constitutes a rope's structure. The structure can affect the rope's abrasion resistance, stretch, flexibility, handgrip, appearance, and many other qualities.

The material used to make cordage also has a significant effect on the properties of the knots you can tie with it. How expensive a rope is, what it looks like, and how it feels to the touch are all dependent on what type of material it is made of. A useful way to consider the properties of rope materials is to break down cordage into natural and synthetic categories.

Twisted Ropes

One of the most basic cordage structures is the twisted rope. Twisting rope to combine fibers was, for a long time, the most common way of making rope. Without machinery, it is the most straightforward way to gather fibers and combine them into rope. A common type of twisted rope is a three-strand rope (**FIGURE 2-1**), which combines three strands that may, in turn, have been twisted from three yarns, each made up of multiple fibers. Other twisted ropes are made of four or more strands, with a small hollow space at the core.

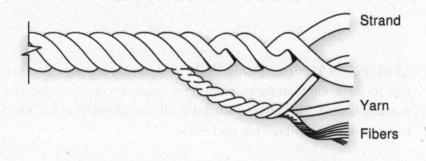

Strand

Yarn

Fibers

FIGURE 2-1: Structure of a three-strand rope

To make a three-strand rope, fibers are twisted in a right-handed fashion to make up yarns, which are combined and twisted together in left-handed fashion to make up strands. Then, the strands are twisted together to the right to make three-strand rope. Rope made by switching the twisting direction with each level is known as "hawser-laid" rope. If hawser-laid rope is made up of three three-stranded ropes that are twisted left-handed, the result is called "cable-laid" rope.

Why twist each succeeding component of the rope in the opposite direction? There's a good explanation: It is constructed in such a way for stability, because the tendency of the rope to untwist will be canceled out if each level of the rope is twisted in the opposite direction.

Direction of the Slant

When the final strands are twisted right-handed, the result is called "Z-laid" rope. This is the same orientation that the threads on an ordinary right-handed screw or bolt would have. When the strands are laid left-handed, the rope is called "S-laid." These designations are due to the direction of slant of the middle part of these letters. This direction must be noted when winding on a whipping as shown in Chapter 12. For greater security, the direction of the winding should be opposite to the direction of the twist.

 FACT

Many knots and knotting techniques came into use as a consequence of the three-strand construction of rope. People began making "multistrand" knots by separating the three strands and combining them to form a knot. Sometimes these strands were even woven back into the rope itself, as in the Back Splice or the Eye Splice. This "splicing" of rope is sometimes done with other types of rope, but it must be done differently for each structure, with widely varying degrees of difficulty.

By its nature, twisted rope's behavior is affected by the direction of its lay. It should be coiled in right-handed fashion as shown in Chapter 12, and will be troublesome if coiled otherwise. This is because the lay of the rope will resist being tightened more than being loosened. It has a slight springiness due to its tendency to untwist under strain, and this causes a load to spin when suspended freely with twisted rope.

Braided and Plaited Ropes

More recently, the use of modern machinery and synthetic fibers has helped us move beyond the limitations of twisted ropes. Rope-making machines can now weave braided or plaited ropes that come in many decorative patterns, are tightly woven, and don't untwist easily like twisted ropes do.

Braid-on-Braid Ropes

One example of a braided rope is a "double braid" or "braid-on-braid" rope, illustrated in **FIGURE 2-2**. This structure is commonly used on more expensive rope, and it is favored for running rigging on sailing vessels due to its excellent knot-holding quality and the way it flattens somewhat to help it grip the surface of a sailing winch.

FIGURE 2-2: Structure of braid-on-braid rope

Unlike twisted rope or many other types of braided rope, braid-on-braid structure has a core that is protected by its outer braid, or sheath. This protection of the core is desirable, but can sometimes make it difficult to detect possible damage. Some "sheath and core" ropes have cores that are not braided but may have any one of many possible structures, even three-strand rope. The core material may be different than the outer sheath, depending on the properties chosen by the manufacturer. The outer sheath may also be chemically treated for particular properties, such as resistance to abrasion or ultraviolet light.

Solid Braid Ropes

When eight, twelve, or even sixteen strands are braided together, resulting in a rope of filled and round cross section (as you can see in **FIGURE 2-3**), it is called "braided" or "solid braid" rope. When the pattern of braiding causes the cross section to be not quite circular, the rope may be called "plaited." With this type of weave, every strand passes along the surface as well as through the center of the rope.

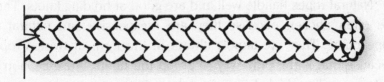

FIGURE 2-3: Structure of a solid braid rope

A Variety of Options

The patterns for braided and plaited rope are endless. Some use strands of different colors, and large plaited dock ropes are sometimes even made of strands twisted in opposing directions to make the final product less susceptible to kinks. Some, like polypropylene ski ropes, consist of just a sheath with no core, giving it an easy-to-splice structure similar to finger cuffs. You can even make a braided rope yourself with a pattern like the Three-Strand Braid (described in Chapter 10).

The pattern of weave alone does not determine all the properties the rope will have. Sometimes the fibers are cut into short lengths to give the rope a fuzzy surface for an easier handhold. How tightly the weave is laid affects the flexibility and stretch the rope will have, and of course the material used will determine many of the rope's properties.

Natural Fiber Ropes

Ropes have been made out of natural fibers since before recorded history, and they still have a place in modern production. Fibers of natural rope are partly plant cellulose, and their stiffness and limited length give natural rope its somewhat harsh and fuzzy look and feel. Because of their plant origins, natural fiber ropes are susceptible to rot from mold and mildew, and should be stored in a dry location. They can also be damaged by oils, acids, and other solvents. Some ropes are conditioned with chemical additives to make them less susceptible to these agents.

Natural ropes handle well and are good at holding knots. They are often chosen because they are inexpensive and natural in appearance. They are almost always in the form of twisted rope, because that is the only way to group the fibers. An exception is cotton or silk, which has a fine enough structure to be spun at thread size and can be woven.

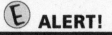 **ALERT!**

> If natural ropes are to be used where safety is a concern, the rope must be evaluated for condition. Even a 1-inch-thick rope can fail to hold a person's weight if it is weathered or aged—even if it does not look "that worn." It's true that you can tell something about a three-strand rope's condition by slightly untwisting it to look at its center, but it's best to know a rope's history of use and abuse and make a judgment call accordingly.

Fibers Stiff and Soft

The stiffer and rougher fibers of larger ropes are usually made from the leaves of manila and sisal. Manila is darker, stronger, and more expensive then sisal; it weathers better than other natural fiber ropes, but should still be dried before storing, even if it has been chemically treated for protection.

Softer fibers are made from the stems of plants like jute, flax, or hemp. These are seldom used in larger ropes anymore. Jute appears as inexpensive garden twine and in decorative cords, and hemp is often used for small jewelry cord, which gets smoother over time when worn as a bracelet.

Cotton is being replaced by synthetics but still appears as both large and small cordage. It is used in handling farm animals because it is smooth and does not burn skin with repeated rubbings nearly as much as other rope materials. Both cotton and silk are used in small sizes for decorative purposes.

Ⓔ FACT

Early in the Great Age of Sail, ropes were made of hemp and were dipped in hot tar for weather protection. When manila became widely available, rope manufacturers were quick to adopt it because it didn't require tar dipping. However, sailors still needed to apply tar to a ship's rigging on a regular basis, especially over the parts lower and closer to the water.

Synthetic Ropes

The second half of the twentieth century brought chemistry into rope manufacture and with it a wide variety of synthetic rope materials. The fibers are made to any length desired and are built of long chain molecules in various formulas. Most synthetic ropes are at least twice as strong as equal-sized natural fiber ropes, and many are even stronger.

Another advantage to using synthetic ropes is that rot and fungus are not as much of a problem, so the ropes do not have to be dried as thoroughly for storage, and in general they weather much better. This is why they are used almost exclusively in boating and rescue applications. But even though synthetic ropes handle and knot well, the general slipperiness of synthetic cordage makes for less security in knot holding; extra care must be taken that a given knot will hold.

There are other concerns as well. Synthetic ropes are more susceptible to degradation from sunlight than natural fiber materials and are sometimes chemically treated to mitigate this. Also, because of their chemical makeup, most synthetic ropes will melt near heat, and they can even melt from the friction of a knot tightening quickly under a load. Some people like to melt the ends of a rope with a lighter to keep them from fraying. This can also be done as a test to distinguish natural from synthetic ropes, since natural fibers burn and char, but do not melt. You may think that you can distinguish between a natural and a synthetic rope, but that's not always the case. Synthetic ropes come in a wide variety of textures and colors, many of which mimic natural fiber ropes.

Ⓔ **ESSENTIAL**

Some activities require rope to meet very precise standards. For pursuits such as mountain climbing or rigging a sailboat, the cordage should meet with specific guidelines to ensure safety. To find out whether a particular type of rope fits the requirement, contact the rope manufacturer.

Nylon Cordage

The term *nylon,* like most terms for synthetic materials, actually refers to more than one formula or specific material of similar properties. Nylon cordage is used in cordage of all sizes from large mooring cables to fishing line and thread. It is somewhat elastic, and hence can absorb more energy from shock loading (temporary tension when the rope comes under sudden strain) than other materials. It is one of the stronger synthetics, sinks in water, and is slightly weaker when wet.

Polyester Cordage

Polyester, also known as Terylene and Dacron, is similar to nylon because it's nearly as strong, but it has much less stretch. It has better resistance to acids and sunlight, and also sinks in water. Polyester ropes are often used in boating and other applications where little stretch and less resistance to shock loading are required.

Polypropylene and Polyethylene Cordage

Polypropylene and polyethylene both float in water, and polypropylene is a favored material for water rescue and water ski ropes. They are both weaker than nylon or polyester, but still stronger by weight than natural fiber ropes. They are both very sensitive to heat, with polyethylene being quite flammable. Both must be protected from prolonged exposure to sunlight, and both are used in inexpensive general utility ropes.

FACT

Because synthetic cordage materials are more slippery than natural fiber, you must put more thought into choosing the right knot for a particular job and spend more time testing the knot for security. Some long-trusted knots like the Bowline can slip when tied with particular kinds of synthetic rope (synthetic ropes vary greatly in their knot holding, so each case may be different). To be sure your rope will hold, you need to try knotting with different types of synthetic ropes.

Other Options

Many other synthetic materials are in use and continue to be developed. High-performance fiber ropes, such as Kevlar and Spectra, are stronger per weight than steel. These and other varieties of high-modulus fibers, though more expensive, offer unique properties for special applications. Detailed information about these new offerings can be obtained from the manufacturers.

Many activities use a very narrow range of rope materials, and you should refer to information sources on those applications to determine what is used. All the properties of rope materials affect the suitability of ropes for given applications, and with a little knowledge you will be able to take them into account for your cordage needs.

Choosing the Right Rope

When it comes to most activities that require the making of knots, whether it is in sailing or decorative arts or another area, it is helpful to understand how the properties of the rope you choose to use affect your application. Some ropes have a very specific application, while others are general-purpose. Not all ropes can be used correctly and safely for any activity. When you choose your rope, consider its properties and how they apply to your particular needs.

Strength under Strain

You need to know the strain that an application will place on the rope and whether this strain will be steady or variable. A steady load is one where the tension will remain constant, such as when binding something that will not shift or suspending something that will not move. Here the strength needed can be as easy to determine as just looking at the weight that is being lifted. However, if the load will not be steady, the strain on the rope will be higher and more difficult to determine.

A shifting load can increase the strain on a rope and can lead to shock loading. You can try to prevent shock loading by securing the load to prevent it from shifting, but sometimes shock loading cannot be avoided and must be accounted for in determining the strength of the rope needed. The less stretch a rope has, the stronger it has to be to resist shock loading; a rope with more stretch can absorb more of the energy of the shock, and therefore doesn't need to be as strong.

Ⓔ ALERT!

One way to deal with shock loading is to use a rope strong enough to provide for a margin of safety. When rope is too weak for the sudden load it receives, a number of problems may occur. The rope may break, it may be weakened due to strain, and any knots that were tied in it may overheat or even melt as a result of the friction caused by being rapidly tightened. Also, if a fitting the rope is secured to is not strong enough, it may break free and fly through the air like a missile.

Rope is best used at or below its "working load" level. Using a rope near its breaking strength will cause what is called "fatigue," and the rope will have lower strength as a result. The working load rating is many times less than its breaking strength and is often labeled on rope packaged for sale. This is the amount of load that can be used on the rope repeatedly without causing fatigue.

As important as strength is to your choice of rope, it may actually be the last criteria that you use. That is because most ropes come in many sizes. You may choose a rope based on other factors such as whether or not it floats, its durability, tendency toward stretch, and so on. After narrowing your choice down to a single type or rope, just choose the size that corresponds to the strength needed.

Ⓔ QUESTION?

How do I determine the strength of a rope?
The rope's strength is determined by the area or cross section of the rope. An otherwise identical rope with twice the diameter will have four times the strength, and vice versa. Moreover, the bigger rope will have less stretch when put under the same amount of strain as the smaller one.

Stretch under Strain

Ropes vary in how much they stretch under strain. Some applications require very little stretch, while some benefit from it. Nylon is an example of a cordage material that stretches, and polyester is a common material used in low-stretch applications. A low-stretch rope can help you avoid shock loading in an object by firmly holding it in place.

Some applications can only use ropes of low stretch. If the rope holding up a sail on a sailboat were able to stretch when the wind picked up, it would allow the sail to move and thus change shape. A hammock should be made of, or slung from, low-stretch materials in order to keep it from sagging to the ground when occupied. Some people want a little stretch in their anchor line to help prevent sudden jerks in the line, causing the anchor to break free. Some fishing lines are made to stretch, which helps keep them from breaking under sudden tension, and some have very little stretch for extra sensitivity. When using ropes and twine that stretch, some of the stretch must be taken out if it is to be tightened. This is easily done with a Trucker's Hitch or another adjustable tie. Some applications require very little stretch and very little "creep," the tendency of a rope to stretch slowly when under continuous tension. Steel cable is often used for this.

Additional Rope Properties

Some properties have to do with the type of abuse the rope will take. Abrasion resistance is sometimes needed, or resistance to ultraviolet rays, insects, mildew, heat, high voltage, rough handling, and repeated knotting. If appearance is important, then you would choose rope based on structure, material, color, surface texture, or size. Other factors may include cost, availability, ease of splicing, quality, tradition, or uniformity with similar uses. Rope can be biodegradable, edible, flammable, glow in the dark, or electrically lighted. If you can't find what you want, you can even make your own!

Sometimes you will have to make do with the rope you have on hand or any substitute you can find. Keeping the properties of rope in mind will help you to make the best use of it. There are knots that can collect the ends of many strands, or that are useful for tying together ropes of very different materials, sizes, and structures. There are also knots that can be tied in bungee cords, straps, sheets, or torn clothing.

The properties of knots do not stand alone, but depend on the substance they are tied in. Keeping this in mind as you learn from this book will make you less frustrated, and a much more competent and safe knot tyer.

3

Learning to Tie Knots

IF YOU WORRY THAT TYING KNOTS is going to be difficult to learn, this chapter should help you get the most out of your efforts. With a little work, you will soon find that it is not difficult to use rope and twine to make any knot you want.

Book Learning

Learning knots from a book can increase your knotting skill in many ways. You can study many new knots, of course, but you may be surprised at how much you can learn about knots you already tie. Even for knots you are already familiar with, you can learn the following:

- Alternative tying methods
- New applications
- Tips for tightening
- Tips for untying
- Safety information
- Historical information

Learning from Diagrams
Although both illustrations and text convey much information in knot books, it is the illustrations that intimidate most people.

There is no need to break out into a cold sweat from the seeming complexity of knot-tying diagrams. Learning knots from diagrams is a skill in itself, and you may be surprised at how easily it is acquired with practice.

It is important to remember that a diagram is only a representation of a knot. It is simply a guide that you will translate into what you do with your hands and the cordage. What may initially look like a complicated diagram may be a knot that is quickly tied with just a couple of twists and tucks. As you progress through the steps of tying a knot, one of the most important things you will learn is how to hold the partially completed knot. As you practice, this will quickly improve.

There is not always a best way to hold a knot while tying it. Sometimes it is just a matter of whatever works best for you. If you watch what your fingers do while you tie your shoes or tie some other knot, you may find you have a very specific way that you hold them during the process of tying.

It Takes Practice

While learning the knot, you may find it much easier to start with a practice rope in a manageable size, especially if you will end up tying the knot in large bulky cordage or with something small, like fishing line. After obtaining some proficiency with the practice rope, you will want to go on to the final material that will be used.

Once you make the switch, you may have to modify the way you hold the rope, the strength you need to apply to bending it, and whether or not you need to wear gloves (if you're handling rough cordage). If you're tying a hitch, you may hold it differently depending on what you are tying it to. For these reasons, it is good to practice the knot with conditions similar to how you will be using it.

You may even decide to carry around a piece of practice cord with you to use whenever you have free moments during the day. You can work on specific techniques, like figuring out how best to snug down the knot, how to tie it quickly, and maybe even how to tie it without looking. Your skill can improve quite a bit just from practicing while you're stuck in traffic (if you're not at the wheel!) or waiting at the doctor's office.

⒠ ESSENTIAL

It is best to practice a knot under conditions as close as possible to its actual use. If you are practicing the Cleat Hitch for tying up a boat, you will want to practice while keeping your fingers from coming too close to the cleat. This will help protect them from being caught when the boat surges on waves and yanks on the line.

Keeping It All Straight

One of the first impressions an inexperienced knot tyer gets when thumbing through the many diagrams of a knot book is that it's all too much information to remember. Perhaps it is all the seemingly indistinguishable crossings. But in practice, you'll soon notice that each knot takes on very distinctive features that you will come to remember almost without trying.

Shared Similarities

One of the first things you will discover after learning a few knots is that they have many similar steps. This means you have much fewer steps to remember. And the more you become familiar with knots, the more these similarities become apparent. Similarities between knots can take on many forms, but the important thing to understand about any knot is that if you change anything about it, you must consider it to be a completely different knot, with its own complete set of properties.

There are a number of ways that different knots can be almost identical. There could be just one tuck that is over rather than under. The difference could come from how you tie it or, for example, if you were to twist a loop in an opposite direction before finishing. Even putting the strain on a different lead or, in the case of a loop, a different pair of leads will result in a new knot.

 **FACT**

> Remembering how to drive to a new address is easy if you already know how to get to a place that is close by. Sometimes it is the same way with learning new knots. You may begin by tying a knot you already know and then just adding or changing something!

The more you come to understand the similarities and differences between knots, the better you will both remember and understand the wide diversity of knot tying. And with the addition of a little practice, you will take advantage of these things without even thinking about it.

Relying on Repetition

Have you ever noticed that sometimes you can only remember a phone number by actually dialing it? It seems as if the memory for the number is in your fingers. This was happening to knot tyers long before there were telephones around. Some tyers can only remember how to tie a knot by actually going through the motions of tying it. Their hands play an important part in retaining their knotting memory.

Of course, you already know that repeating something helps you remember it, but you might be amazed at how efficiently this works with knot tying. And with practice, your hand motions become more efficient and effective, which also aids memory. After a time, you'll be able to tie a knot without even thinking about it. It is best not to carry this to an extreme. It is actually possible to have trouble remembering a knot if you "overthink" it. This happens sometimes when tying neckties, where you could have trouble remembering it if you are paying attention. One way to avoid this is to consciously think about the knot while learning it. That way, you'll be more aware of its structure and how you hold it while tying.

Ⓔ ALERT!

> If you are using a knot where safety is at stake, it is crucial that you follow all the steps of tying it correctly. Make sure that the strain is on the appropriate leads coming from the knot. Any change to which leads get strain or even the direction of the strain will result in a different knot with different properties, which may slip or jam.

Sometimes a knot must be remembered in a hurry or while you're distracted. This is often the case for people who use rope in emergency services or when sailing. Under stressful circumstances, a person will tie based on habit. You should practice your tying as closely as possible to the conditions you will have when in a hurry and under stress, and use repetition. If you do anything differently when you practice—for example, making a loop too small or not tightening it all the way—you will probably tie it that way when you need it quickly or under pressure.

As you work through the process of learning and practicing with knots, memory will come naturally. You will also come to associate different types of knots with different applications, and thus will quickly be able to choose the correct knot for the job. So just have fun learning, and the memory part will take care of itself.

Tips for Tying

There are a number of things you can do to help make learning knots more successful and enjoyable. Gaining experience with following the diagrams presented in this book and other publications will help. Choosing a good practice cord can make your task easier. And sharing your knowledge can make learning more fun, too.

Choosing a Good Practice Cord

Beginners often overlook the importance of finding the right practice cord. Remember, choosing a good piece or two of practice cord can greatly enhance the time you spend tying the knot. It should be thick enough to be seen clearly and thin enough to manipulate easily. It should be flexible, hold a knot, and yet not jam readily. A good test is to tie the cord you've picked out in an Overhand Knot and put it under moderate strain, then see if it unties easily. If it jams, it will be awkward to work with. Also check if the cordage material you plan to use is spongy—it will make untying difficult because the knot will shrink when tightened. And if the cordage is too slippery, it will be more difficult to hold in position while tying.

For tying bends—joining one cord to another—it helps to use two cords of different color, because it'll be easy for you to distinguish them from each other. And it may not hurt to consider which colors will work best. Certain colors make it easier to see knot structure, and using solid-colored cords is always better than multicolored ones.

ⓔ QUESTION?

Where can I buy a good cord for practicing knots?
Many stores have their cordage on large spools where you can try it out. Tie and untie a couple of knots with each type of rope to see how they feel. See which color you like best for tying. A small solid-braid halyard from a marine store is an example of a good practice cord.

Also make sure you get a piece of cordage long enough to sustain the types of knots you plan to practice. For instance, knots with multiple loops will need to be longer than knots like a Figure Eight Knot. One option is to get a couple of cords of different lengths.

It is sometimes easier to practice fishing knots with a larger cord before tying them in fishing line. Because of the way some of these knots are tightened, the more flexible the cord, the better. A good example is the very flexible type of miniblind cord. When you are confident that you are tying it correctly, you can try it with small clear fishing line. It may also be safer to practice tying to something less sharp than a fishhook while you are first learning.

Tips for Following Illustrations

Any illustration can be followed correctly, as long as you have some patience. One way to get practice is to follow the diagram of a knot you already know. If you are having difficulty holding the shape of the knot before you are finished tying it, try pinning it down on a corkboard or over a photocopy of the diagram (you might want to use a copy machine to enlarge the diagram). Most of the knots have the same behavior if the image of the diagram is reversed, so a left-handed person may have less difficulty tying from a reversed image.

Laying out multiple cords to match the stages of an illustration can help, too. Be especially careful that the loops you make have the same crossings at the base as in the illustration. You can also try drawing the diagram yourself to help understand the crossings. If you are still having trouble, learning similar knots could help set you straight. Be sure to read the text accompanying the knot. If you can, get someone to help you.

Additional Considerations

Most knots will only demonstrate their correct behavior when they are tightened down to their proper form. Until this is done, the knot is only a tangle with the proper crossings! It is usually best to pull on all the leads coming from a knot, and with a little practice and experimentation, you can learn to do this with minimal tugs. Some knots can end up with the wrong form if they are not tightened correctly, so this is very important.

Once a knot is tightened, it will have a distinctive look. By learning to recognize this look, you can often judge if it is tied correctly with just a glance. With a little experimentation you will also discover that many knots untie easily when done a certain way. Some knots, like the Hunter's Bend, are quickly loosened by bending back the outer collar (the part of the knot that the standing part leads out of).

Ⓔ ESSENTIAL

Much of our terminology for ropes and knots comes from what is called "the age of sail." That's because many of the first books that referred to knots were early sailing and seamanship guides. Many of the terms we use today are due to their first appearance in these sailing books.

Knots by Name

When it comes to learning from a knot book, knowing some basic terminology is key. Knots have names, different functions that knots serve have names, and even the parts of a knot have names. Once you learn all these terms, you will find that learning and remembering knots will be much easier.

The term *knot,* in its most general definition, can refer to any complication in rope that has the potential for the rope to act differently than if it were not there. Since there is no official registry for the names of knots, they tend to be named by convention, by what the majority of books call them, or just by what a father called it when he taught it to his son. These names come from many sources:

- A profession or application that relies on the knot
- The knot's form or function
- The knot's inventor, famous user, or another person

Many knots have more than one name, and sometimes one name has been applied to more than one knot. When working with other people, it is sometimes necessary to double-check that you are in fact talking about the same knot when you refer to it simply by name.

Knotting Functions

Different types of knots have different functions. A brief summary here will help you see at a glance the different jobs done by knots and the terms used to describe them.

The term *bend* refers to a knot that is used to join one rope to another. This is normally done when one rope needs to be longer, or when one type of rope needs to be fastened to another type. The term *hitch* is used to describe a knot that attaches a rope to an object, like a ring, bar, or post.

Other types of knots are stopper knots, loop knots, binding knots, and decorative knots:

- **Stopper knot:** A knot tied in the end of a cord.
- **Loop knot:** A knot that makes a circle or loop out of cord.
- **Binding knot:** A knot that uses cordage to bind one or more items.
- **Decorative knot:** A knot that is tied for its appearance.

Knot-Tying Terms

Knowing a few terms for knot tying is very important for following both illustrations and descriptions in the text. When you work with a rope, it generally has a standing part, bight, and running end (**FIGURE 3-1**).

When a knot is tied at the end of a rope, the very tip is referred to as the "running end." In fishing publications, this section may be referred to as the "tag end." Using this term in knotting directions gives the important distinction that the very tip of the rope is delivered where the directions say, whether it is over or under another rope, or through a loop of some kind. The other end of the rope—the leading part that is not manipulated in the knot tying—is called the "standing part."

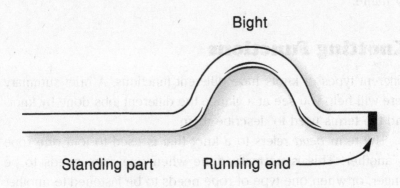

FIGURE 3-1: Standing part, bight, and running end

The term "bight" is the middle part of the rope that is not the running end or standing part. Just as a running end can be directed in many ways in the construction of a knot, a bight can be made out of any part of the rope, and directed the same way. If an arrow in an illustration seems to come from the standing part and not from the running end, it usually means that a bight should be formed and taken in the direction the arrow shows. It may help with some knots to fold the bight over very tight, thus forming a narrow doubled piece that can pass more easily where needed.

The Crossing Turn

Another important structure in knot tying is the crossing turn, used in many of the knots you'll learn in this book. You can quickly create a crossing turn by grabbing a part of the bight and giving it a half twist that forms a loop, as seen in **FIGURE 3-2**. When making a crossing turn, it is very important that the orientation of the over-under section of the crossing is correct for the knot you are tying. In practice, you will quickly get the crossing orientation correct each time by associating it with a twist in a certain direction, which is quicker than trying to think about whether the running end crosses over or under when producing it.

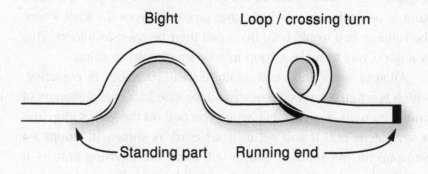

FIGURE 3-2: The crossing turn

Hitching Practices

When you tie a knot in the rope without ever using the running end, you're said to "tie in the bight." Tying in the bight may be done in the middle of the rope or near the end (as long as you're not moving the running end). For example, you can make a Clove Hitch by making two crossing turns in the bight, as shown in **FIGURE 3-3**. Then, lay the right crossing turn over the left one, and the resulting hitch can then be placed over the end of a post.

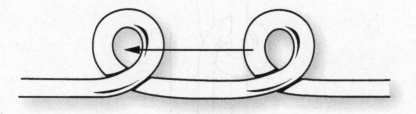

FIGURE 3-3: Two crossing turns for a Clove Hitch

Many knots that are usually tied with the running end can be tied in the bight by folding a bight anywhere in the line and then using it exactly as you would a running end. When a Simple Overhand Knot is tied this way, the bight that protrudes from the knot where the running end would have been can then be used as a loop. This is a good way to make a loop in very small cord or string.

Another term important in understanding knots is *capsizing*, which is when a knot changes its shape due to a rearrangement of one of its parts—for example, when you pull on the knot's loop and it straightens out. If you set up your cord as shown in **FIGURE 3-4** and pull on the running end, it will leave the crossing turn as it straightens and another crossing turn will form on the cord that was running through it. This transformation can happen in knots when they are not snugged down into their proper form, causing the knot to "spill." In the case of the Square or Reef Knot, this is done intentionally, to untie it more quickly (capsizing is sometimes done on purpose to aid in tying a knot).

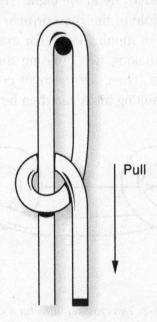

Pull

Figure 3-4: Pulling on the running end will capsize the knot

When you're making hitches, you'll also come across "turns" and "round turns." These are two ways of starting a hitch around a ring, bar, or rail (see **FIGURE 3-5**). With the turn, the running end is passed just once around the rail, which will allow a transfer of strain from the standing part to the rest of the knot. This may be desirable for some hitches that are better able to hold with strain on them. With the round turn, the extra turn around the rail allows friction to help hold against strain in the standing part, which may help when hitching a rope under strain and takes some of the strain off the knot. The round turn is the first part of the popular hitch called the Round Turn and Two Half Hitches.

FIGURE 3-5: Starting a hitch: turn and round turn

Tying Overhand

The Overhand Knot and the Multiple Overhand Knot structures are used in many knots, and it is valuable to become familiar with their form. **FIGURE 3-6** shows the shape of a Multiple Overhand Knot of three turns in what is called its "belly and spine" form (the belly may also be referred to as the bight). When you tighten the Multiple Overhand Knot by pulling on both ends, the belly wraps around the spine until it is barrel-shaped, as shown in **FIGURE 3-7**.

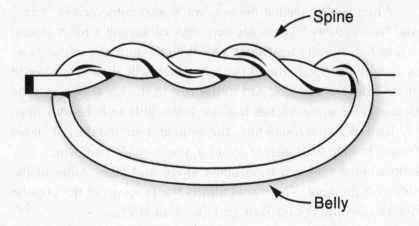

Spine

Belly

FIGURE 3-6: Multiple Overhand Knot in "belly and spine" form

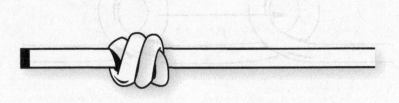

FIGURE 3-7: Completed Multiple Overhand Knot in barrel shape

The Right Knot for Any Job

When you open up a drawer or box of tools, it is immediately obvious that some of them are right and some of them are wrong for the job you have in mind. When you have a job to do with rope, the knots you know will serve you as your toolbox. Just as you would not have much use for a toolbox with just one tool in it, you would not want to do different jobs with rope or string with just one knot. You will want to learn a few different types of knots and learn to use the right one for your application.

Matching a Knot to a Rope Application

The main categories of rope use are joining one rope to another, making a loop, binding, and tying off to an object. Identifying the function that the knot must serve is an important step in choosing one. Some knots are like a multitool in that they can serve a variety of functions, and some are very limited in what they do. A fixed loop can serve a variety of different functions, but a knot like the Reef or Square Knot is unreliable when not used as a binding knot. Once you understand the function of the knot you learn, you will know whether it will work in any particular application.

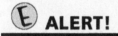 **ALERT!**

Don't be quick to assume that a knot you like and trust in one application will behave reliably in another. Many knots that are very good for one application can quickly untie or slip when used in only a slightly different manner. Just as you wouldn't use a good pair of pliers to drive a nail through wood, you need to discriminate between appropriate and inappropriate knots for each application.

Other Considerations

The more you learn about knots, the more factors you will be able to take into account as you choose the right one for a particular application. Everything from the cordage material used to how the knot is tied, untied, and subjected to stress are important factors in knot choice.

No attempt is made in this book to tell you what rope material to use for every application. That is because only you will know both what application you have and what cordage you have available to do it. That leaves you to decide what knots to use based on the rope's properties, such as its size and how slippery it is.

There are many questions to ask yourself when choosing a knot for a given application:

- Will the rope be under steady or changing strain?
- Will it need to be untied?
- Will it need to be tied or untied quickly?
- What knots do I know?
- How secure does it need to be?
- Will others need to tie or untie it?
- Will the tension in the rope need to be adjusted later?
- Will others have to use it?
- Is damaging the rope a concern?

These and many other questions can come into play when you choose a knot. You will, of course, need to limit your choices to which knots you know, just as you must choose from your toolbox only tools that are in it. This leads us to another question you may have been wondering about: "Which knots should I learn?"

Ⓔ FACT

Even if you read that it is good to use ¼-inch-diameter rope for securing loads on the back of a pickup, you will probably still find yourself getting ready to haul purchases away from a lumber yard with thin and slippery tomato twine to secure it. For situations like these, it is good to have knowledge of different knots to get the job done with a variety of materials.

Choosing Which Knots to Learn

Many people are quite intimidated by the thought of learning more than just a couple of knots, or think that it is difficult or time-consuming. So here are some things to ponder when deciding which ones you want to learn.

The first thing you may wonder about is how many knots you will need to know or what is the smallest number that you can get by on. The number is up to you and may vary depending on your needs. Here is a possible progression you might consider: A loop knot like the Bowline or Overhand Loop can serve a number of different applications, and thus gets you the most mileage from a single knot. Next you should consider learning other knots from different categories, like bends, hitches, and binding knots, so that you can apply them to many situations. It is better still to learn a couple of knots from each category. You might try experimenting with a number of knots within a given category, and settle on the ones you want to remember and use.

Many knots are similar in structure, which means that the more different kinds of knots you learn to make, the easier it'll be to add new knots to your stock. Because of this, you may decide to choose knots from different categories that have similar structure—you'll be able to remember them more easily. For example, the multiple overhand structure appears in many knots throughout this book, and so do knots that make use of combinations of Half Hitches.

Ⓔ **ESSENTIAL**

There is a lot of room in knot tying for personal preference. You can decide to pay extra attention to knots that are adjustable, knots that allow leverage, knots that untie very easily after being under heavy strain, knots that are very secure, or even knots that are decorative as well as functional. Some people enjoy exploring and learning knots that exhibit these or other particular properties.

Taking time to learn tips for learning knots, especially learning the terminology, is key to success at learning new knots. Not only does practice help in tying knots, but it helps in following diagrams and in learning knots more easily. With a little work, you will have no trouble both tying and teaching many of the different knots in this book. The chapters that follow include many types of knots, and even tips on teaching them and exploring the subject further.

4

Stopper Knots

THE BEST PLACE TO START LEARNING KNOTS is with stopper knots, or knots that are tied at the end of a cord. Stopper knots have many uses and provide an excellent learning base for practicing a wide variety of other knots.

Stopping and More

Stopper knots, also known as terminal knots or knob knots, are tied at the end of a cord. In its strictest sense, the use of the word *knot* refers to a stopper knot.

A rope with a knot tied in the end of it is a completely different object than a rope without one. It is easier to hang on to, it cannot be pulled through the same size openings, the end will be less inclined to come unraveled, and it will look different, too. All these changes in the properties of the rope are accomplished with a simple stopper knot.

Basic Usage

To stop a cord's end from running through a small opening is part of how a stopper knot earns its name. By "stopping" the rope, the knot allows us to suspend something from it. If the cord runs through a lead or pulley, a stopper knot can keep the line from running all the way out, or unreeving. This is commonly done on a sailboat, where the Figure Eight Knot is used for this purpose. It also stops the end of thread from passing through cloth and similar materials in needlework.

A simple stopper knot is often used to make cordage easier to grasp, whether you make it with the string doubled through the end of a zipper, or with larger rope to get a better grip. Several stopper knots can be tied, and spaced out, to give many handholds. When tied in the end of many cords as if all one cord, it provides a way to keep them gathered.

Ⓔ FACT

Some knots with different names and uses are really the same knot tied under different circumstances. Many loop knots are tied the same as other knots but around their own standing part. The Double Overhand Knot is called the Strangle Knot when it is tied over two crossed sticks, and the Strangle Snare when it is tied around its own standing part.

More Than Just for Stopping

There are many other uses for stopper knots. They can make the end heavier to use for throwing. Heaving knots are for weighting the end of a rope to assist with throwing the rope. Often a smaller rope is thrown between a boat and the dock, and then used to pull a heavier one over. The same technique is used in many circumstances to get a heavy rope in a hard-to-reach place. In getting a rope over and between two particular branches high in a tree, a rope can be thrown over all of them, and then another can be thrown across it between the branches, from a different angle, 90 degrees if possible. In this manner, the second rope will pull the first down between the two branches. Two common knots for weighting the end of a line are the Heaving Line Knot and the Monkey's Fist.

Stopper knots can be used as mallets with a soft striking surface, or they can be treated with shellac to harden them. They also use up line to make it shorter. Both the Heaving Line Knot and the Monkey's Fist have a number of turns that use up line. Depending on how much shorter a cord needs to be, anything can be used from an Overhand Knot to a long Heaving Line Knot or even a coil. They can prevent the end from fraying, although whipping the end, as shown in Chapter 12, is a neater solution. Stopper knots are used for decoration, and a knot in the end of a cord can be used as a reminder of something.

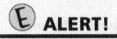 **ALERT!**

The Monkey's Fist can be dangerous if it hits a bystander while throwing it to a dock or a person trying to catch it. This is especially true if extra weight is added in the middle of it. Sometimes a small bag of sand is used to weight the end of a line if there is risk of injury.

Multistrand Stopper Knots

Knot tyers long ago figured out that the strands of three-stranded rope can be unlayed and then tied together to form simple or complex stopper knots. These knots are characterized by simple and easy-to-remember patterns for tying, and their woven appearance. On square-rigged sailing ships these knots were used to stop hands and feet from sliding on ropes. They can also be tied by binding two or more separate cords together. Multistrand knots are also used as a form of decorative knot tying. Some knots, like the Matthew Walker Knot, can serve both decorative and functional purposes.

Multistrand stopper knots can be made in many variations just by using the Wall and Crown Knots (described later in this chapter). They can be combined in various orders and can even be doubled to make a larger knot. To double them, retrace each strand along a previous strand's path. If a Wall and then a Crown is made, the ends can be tucked down the center from the top and then cut off where they come out the bottom. Then, when someone asks what you did with the ends, you can say that you "threw them away."

Ⓔ QUESTION?

Why does my attempt at making a Matthew Walker Knot look like a rat's nest?
Tying the Matthew Walker Knot is a good example of a knot that does not form the proper shape just from pulling on all the leads. The outer bights must be coaxed into place to wrap around the knot in the proper form. Gently brush them with your hand to assist them in wrapping all the way around the knot, while gradually and evenly taking out slack.

The Overhand Series

The Overhand Knot is a distinct knot with its own properties. It is also the basis for both tying and remembering many knots (as shown in Chapter 3). For instance, the Overhand Knot is the base for two important series of stopper knots, the figure eight series and the multiple overhand series.

The Figure Eight Series

The figure eight series contains frequently used knots. This series begins by making the crossing turn that would be used for an Overhand Knot, and then increasing the number of times the running end is wrapped around the standing part before passing once through the loop. Twisting this loop an increasing number of times before threading accomplishes the same thing. This series of knots is often used to stop a line from passing through an opening.

The Multiple Overhand Series

The multiple overhand series is made by increasing the number of wraps in the spine of the knot. After making an overhand knot, pass the running end through the loop of the knot multiple times, making a different knot in the series every time.

 FACT

Multiple Overhand Knots are also called Barrel Knots and Blood Knots. There are various explanations for the origin of the term "Blood Knot." One version explains that they were tied in the lashes of floggers to cause them to draw more blood. Another version claims the name comes from causing bleeding fingers from tight knots in a fishing line. And yet another claims that this knot was popular with surgeons.

When tied this way, these knots change shape as they are tightened. If you tighten them by pulling on both the running and standing parts, the belly wraps around the spine until all you can see is the barrel shape of these wraps. They can also be tightened by manually wrapping the belly around the spine, which causes the spine to unwrap to a single crossing. These knots have many properties in common, including both high security and difficulty in untying when tightened.

Another way to tie this series is to make the desired number of wraps, and then pass the running end through all of them, leaving it already in its final form. The Double and Triple Overhand Knots are often tied this way. Knots of this series all have a right- and a left-handed version.

A Starting Place

Knots in the overhand series are the starting point of many other knots, bends, hitches, and loops. Some bends are made by interlocking Overhand Knots, some hitches are started with an

Overhand or Figure Eight, and many friction loops and fishing knots are based on Multiple Overhand Knots.

There are many advantages to tying knots that are based on others. They are certainly easier to remember because there is so much less to recall. By making it easier to keep many possibilities in mind, you can make better choices for what is needed. When one knot is the basis for another, it is also easier to check your progress as you complete the knot.

ⒺESSENTIAL

For both of the series of stopper knots mentioned here, increasing the number of wraps will not give them an increased cross-section area. Continuing past the Figure Eight or the Double Overhand in their series makes the knots longer but not wider. For a wider knot, use a different knot or double the cord first.

Overhand Knot

This knot has several names. You may hear it called Simple Overhand Knot. If you use thread or other small cordage to tie this knot, it is called the Thumb Knot. When tied with two cords, as when you start tying shoelaces, it is called the Half Knot.

 Pass the running end around the standing part, making a loop, and then pass it through the crossing turn.

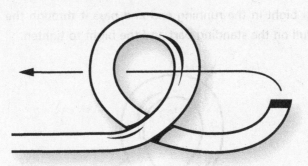

2 Tighten the knot by pulling on both the standing part and the running end.

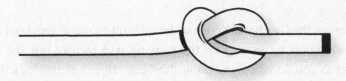

Besides being the foundation of many different knots, the Overhand Knot has many distinct properties of its own. For example, it weakens most cordage it is tied in by 50 percent or more, and tightening it down can damage the fibers of some ropes. Consequently, it is tied in nylon fishing line to test for brittleness. If fishing line has lost any of its flexibility, it will break very easily as you tie an Overhand Knot in it and tighten it with a quick jerk from both sides. Fishermen take care not to accidentally let an Overhand Knot form in their line so as not to lose half its strength. Once it's tied, the knot is difficult to undo. It should only be tied in small cordage or thread if it is not meant to be untied.

Slipped Overhand Knot

You start the Slipped Overhand Knot the same way you begin tying the Overhand Knot, with one variation—the last tuck is made with a bight of the running end, so that the very end is not pulled through the crossing turn. This is what you do when you tie the bows in your shoelaces.

▶ Pass the running end around the standing part, making a loop; then, make a bight in the running end and pass it through the crossing turn. Pull on the standing part and the bight to tighten.

Whereas the Overhand Knot can be difficult to untie, this knot can be untied simply by pulling on the running end to take out the last tuck, just as you do when you untie shoelaces. However, this trick does not work with all knots, as not all knots can be released by letting out the last tuck.

Slipped Noose

This knot is similar to the Slipped Overhand Knot. The difference is that the last tuck is made with a bight of the standing part, instead of the running end.

▶ Pass the running end around the standing part, making a loop; then, make a bight in the standing part and pass it through the crossing turn. Pull on the running end and on the bight loop to tighten.

It is important to learn the difference between the Slipped Overhand Knot and the Slipped Noose. Each one will serve you as the starting point for other knots.

Figure Eight Knot

This knot is started like the Overhand Knot, but here the running end makes a complete round turn around the standing part before passing through its loop.

 Use the running end to make a crossing turn, and pass the end under the standing part.

 Twist the running end up and through the crossing turn.

3 Tighten the knot by pulling on both ends.

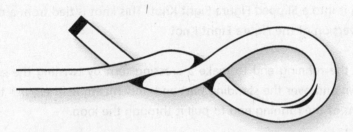

If you wish to use the Figure Eight Knot as a stopper knot, modify Step 2 by pulling the standing part while pressing against the base of the knot on that side. When the Figure Eight Knot and similar stopper knots are tightened this way, the running end will point to the side at a right angle.

The Figure Eight Knot is frequently used as a basis for other knots. It is much easier to untie than the Overhand Knot, and is not as damaging to rope fibers. Because the Figure Eight Knot has a distinctive "figure eight" look, it's easy to check to make sure it's tied correctly. This is one of the reasons it is popular with rescue work. It is used on the running rigging of sailboats to keep lines from running all the way through leads and pulleys.

Slipped Figure Eight Knot

If you want your Figure Eight Knot to release quickly, modify it by making it into a Slipped Figure Eight Knot. This knot is tied from a different version of the Figure Eight Knot.

▶ Use the running end to make a crossing turn by twisting the end down and over the standing part and underneath it. Then, use the bight of the running end to pull it through the loop.

You can release this knot simply by pulling on the running end.

Stevedore Knot

This knot begins like the Overhand, but here the running end makes two complete round turns around the standing part before passing through its loop.

▶ Make a crossing turn with the running end by passing it down, over the standing part, down behind it, up over it, down behind it again, and through the loop. Pull on the standing part and running end to tighten.

The name of this knot refers to the profession of dockworkers, who were said to use this as a stopper knot. Although it is not wider than the Figure Eight, it is bulkier and has a distinctive look when pulled down as a stopper knot. This knot is difficult to pull down to stopper knot form when tied by twisting the crossing turn.

Double Overhand Knot

This knot is the first in the multiple overhand series. It starts with a Simple Overhand Knot, and then the running end is passed through the crossing turn a second time, making the belly-and-spine appearance you see in step 1.

1 Lay down the rope with the running end facing left. Move it down and twist to make the belly, bringing it up over the right side of the standing part.

2 Run the running end up and under the standing part, making two overhand loops.

3 Tighten the knot by pulling on both the standing part and the running end.

Twisting the ends in opposite directions will either help the belly wrap around the spine or impede it, depending on which way they are twisted. The Double Overhand, like all knots in the series, is very secure and difficult to untie.

Triple Overhand Knot

This next knot in the multiple overhand series is tied similarly to the Double Overhand, but with three passes through the loop instead of two. When tied this way, it also has the belly-and-spine appearance you see in step 1.

 Tying this knot, you follow the steps described in the Double Overhead Knot, adding an extra loop at the end.

 When you pull on both ends to tighten the knot, the belly will wrap around the spine, giving the knot its final barrel shape when fully tightened.

(continued)

Triple Overhand Knot (continued)

3 A popular way to tie this knot is to make the wraps working backward along the standing part, and then passing the running end through all the wraps at once.

You will follow the same procedure when tying the Uni-Knot, as described in Chapter 11.

Oysterman's Stopper

The Oysterman's Stopper knot begins by tying the Slipped Noose.

1 Tie a Slip Noose, making a tuck through the loop.

2 Tuck the working end through the noose.

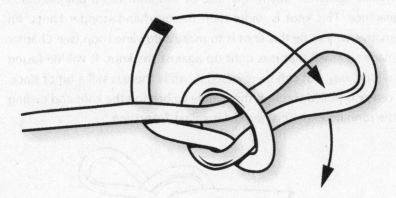

(continued)

Oysterman's Stopper (continued)

3 Pull the standing part to trap the running end with the loop.

4 As you tighten the knot, you should get the finished Oysterman's Stopper.

When tightened down, the face of this knot has a unique trefoil appearance. This knot is wider than the overhand stopper knots. An alternative way to tie this knot is to make a Bowline Loop (see Chapter 6), made so small that it is right up against the knot. It will be facing the wrong way, but can be reversed if, while there is still a bit of slack, the center is pulled through the middle by bracing the knot and pulling on the running end. This reversal is called "capsizing."

Heaving Line Knot

The Heaving Line Knot, also known as the Monk's Knot, gets its name from the heaving line—a smaller line made to heave from a boat to dock so that it can be used to pull a heavier line over.

 Double the line back for the length desired, and then begin tightly wrapping the running end around the doubled-up rope, making concentric circles to the left.

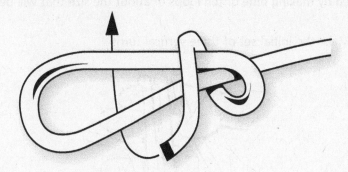

2 As you get to the end, tuck the running end through the last of the remaining bight. Pulling on the standing part will tighten this last tuck in place.

The Heaving Line Knot is useful for shortening a line and for weighting the end for heaving, if necessary. It is also used decoratively.

Monkey's Fist

The Monkey's Fist Knot is most frequently used as a heaving knot, and can even be tied around an object to make it heavier. The knot is also popular with children, and is used as a decorative knot. It is made small to give earrings a nautical look, larger to make key fobs, and larger still to make doorstops. A pair tied to opposite ends of a 2-foot cord makes a good cat toy.

Before you start making the knot, estimate the length of line needed by making nine or ten loops of about the size that will be tied.

1 Make the initial set of three vertical turns.

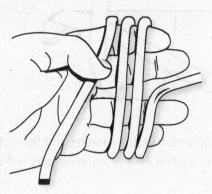

2 Hold the turns in place as you add three horizontal turns.

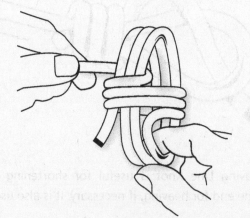

Next, add three turns that go through the middle of the knot, wrapping over the top and around the vertical turns.

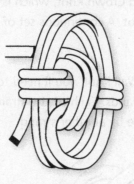

4 Take care that the loops stay in place, and that they continue to stay in place, as you carefully work the slack out through the knot, one turn at a time.

The end can be left long and spliced into the standing part, or tucked into the knot. If the end is to be tucked within the knot, an Oysterman's Stopper tied in the end will help fill its center. After it is pushed into the middle of the knot, work the slack back to the standing part of the cord.

A variation on the Monkey's Fist Knot is to use more than three turns. And for the ambitious knot tyer, a three-turn Monkey's Fist can serve as the center for a five-turn Monkey's Fist, and so forth, tucking each Monkey's Fist inside the new one such that lines stay perpendicular.

Wall Knot

Generally, the Wall Knot is not tied on its own, but is the basis for other knots, such as the Wall and Crown Knot, which is made by first tying a Wall and then a Crown Knot. A continuous set of Wall Knots can cover a cylindrical object.

1 In order to make the Wall Knot, you'll need to separate the end of the rope into three strands. Each of the strands is tucked upward through the loop made by another strand.

2 Tighten the knot by pulling on the strands.

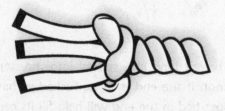

In preparing three-strand rope for multistrand knots, it is best to whip the end of each strand and bind the rope itself with a Constrictor Knot (see Chapter 8) to keep the strands from separating any further down the rope.

Crown Knot

The Crown Knot is very similar to the Wall Knot, except the direction of the running ends, which go down rather than up.

1 Take the three strands of the rope and tuck each one down through the loop made by another strand.

2 Tighten the knot by pulling on the strands.

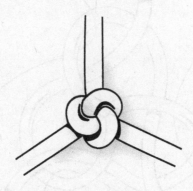

This knot is rarely tied by itself, unless you keep on tying this knot to cover a cylindrical object.

Matthew Walker Knot

This is another decorative knot that requires separating the rope you're working with into three strands.

1 Begin the Matthew Walker Knot by making a Wall Knot, tucking each end up through the next bight.

2 Continue by making another tuck.

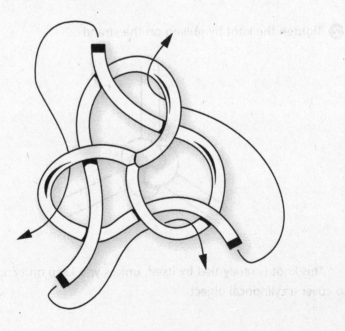

3 Snug down by pulling each of the strands repeatedly.

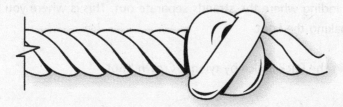

Another way to tie the Matthew Walker Knot is to lay the strands in successive Overhand Knots.

1 Use one strand to make an Overhand Knot.

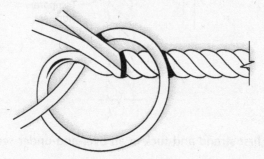

2 Continue making Overhand Knots with each consecutive strand.

As you pull on the strands to tighten the knot, make sure you do it gradually and evenly.

Back Splice

To make a Back Splice, you need to prepare the rope by adding temporary binding where the strands separate out. This is where you will begin making the knot.

1 Begin the Back Splice by tying a Crown Knot.

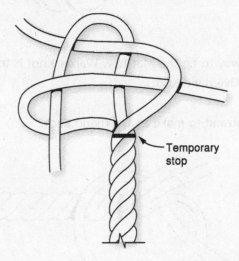

Temporary stop

2 Take the first strand and tuck in an over-and-under sequence.

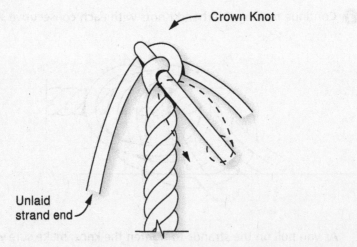

Crown Knot

Unlaid strand end

3 Continue tucks for a minimum of three times.

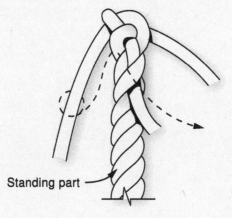

Standing part

4 When you finish, you should have a rope end that looks like this.

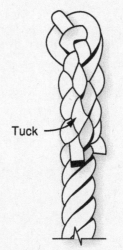

Tuck

The Back Splice Knot is used to keep three-strand rope from fraying and coming apart. If desired, the strands can be partially trimmed after each tuck to taper the splice.

5

Tying Bends

A KNOT USED TO JOIN THE ENDS OF TWO ROPES is called a bend. The knots you will find in this chapter will join cordage small and large, similar and different—a skill that you will find useful in many endeavors.

Uses and Useful Tips

When a bend joins the ends of two ropes, it is to provide more length or make a needed connection. A bend should be considered a temporary join, except in the case of small cordage such as twine or fishing line. You may need a bend to repair a broken rope (keeping in mind that rope is weaker at the knot). You can use a bend to join electrical cords. When the ends are plugged in, they will not pull out if there is tension on the cord.

When used to join the ends of a single rope, a bend makes a circle of rope called a "strop" or "sling." A closed circle of rope can be used for hitching or lifting, such as the Barrel Sling described in Chapter 7.

Bends are characterized by having two standing ends and two running ends. When tightened down, leave enough length of running end to provide security against the ends slipping back through the knot. Depending on the knot, the length of the running end can be anywhere from a few to several times the diameter of the rope. If extra security is desired, the running ends can even be tied around the standing ends of the opposite rope. Anything from a Half Hitch to a Triple Overhand Knot can be used for this purpose.

 **ESSENTIAL**

Do not be surprised that this chapter does not include a Square Knot. Also called the Reef Knot, it is notorious for coming undone when used as a bend. If bumped, it will untie so readily that it is used in magic tricks to give the appearance of "magically" untying two ropes without effort. It is especially unstable if used on ropes of different size or material. If kept flat against a surface, however, it makes a great binding knot, so you will find it in Chapter 8.

Bends vary in how easily they are untied after being under strain. Since ease of untying may or may not be desirable depending on your circumstances, you want to keep this property in mind when you choose your bend. Knots like the Water Knot or the Fisherman's Knot can be very difficult to untie, especially in twine. The Zeppelin Bend can be untied easily even after being subjected to great strain.

Working with Two Dissimilar Ropes

It often happens that the ropes you want to join will be of different size or material. Great care must be taken because most bends have very little security when they are not tied with two identical ropes. There are two ways of dealing with this. One is to use a knot that is somewhat suited for ropes of different size, like the Sheet Bend or the Double Sheet Bend, and the other is to treat the join as if it were a hitch.

The Sheet Bend is commonly used when a rope of larger size is tied to a smaller one. In this case, the larger cord is the one that is bent into a U-shape, as you'll see in the instructions for tying the Sheet Bend later in this chapter. If the size difference is too large, however, this knot will be insecure. To help the join handle a bigger size difference, a Double Sheet Bend can be used. These knots are also popular for ropes that are of different material. For each circumstance, you must tie and test your join to determine its suitability.

 **ALERT!**

Knots that involve combining two or more ropes of different materials can be very unreliable and unpredictable. Not only does the presence of different materials affect the friction within the knot, but different ropes vary in their stiffness and springiness as well, further compromising the ability of a knot to keep its form.

When the size difference of the ropes to be joined is significant, you may not want to tie them together at all, but connect them with loops or hitches. A rope can also be tied to a larger rope with a hitch just as if it were a pole. This is made easier if there is a loop at the end of the larger rope to which a smaller rope can be attached with almost any hitch. A loop can also be tied in each end so that they interlock. The Bowline Bend is such a join and if the loop knots themselves are secure, this join is secure regardless of the differences of the two ropes.

ESSENTIAL

It is important to remember that there is both a left- and a right-handed version of the Overhand Knot. The left-handed Overhand Knot, like the one in Chapter 4, is also known as an "S" Overhand Knot. The right-handed Overhand Knot, like the one at the end of this chapter, called the Overhand Bend, is known as a "Z" Overhand Knot. The letters *S* and *Z* describe the path the running end takes through the spine of the knot. The same is true for Multiple Overhand Knots.

Interlocking Overhand Bends

A type of joining knot worth learning is the Interlocking Overhand Bend. In this type of knot, the end of each rope forms an Overhand Knot, and they are intertwined. Out of the many different joining knots that can be made from Interlocking Overhand Knots, four are shown in this chapter: Ashley's Bend, Hunter's Bend, Zeppelin Bend, and Butterfly Bend. These are all excellent bends, each with its own properties and tying methods.

There are two approaches to tying Interlocking Overhand Knots. One is to tie an Overhand Knot in one end, and then tie an Overhand in the other end while threading this end through the first Overhand. The other method is to ignore the fact that the ends make an Overhand Knot, and just intertwine both ends as needed to make the knot. This is illustrated for each of these four knots in this chapter, along with a figure showing the overhand structure of each.

(E) QUESTION?

How can I tell if I have tied the bend correctly?
Many bends have a distinctive look when they are tightened. You can also try loosening them to the point where the structure is spread out a bit, and then comparing it to a diagram. This is made much easier if the ropes are of different color.

You should try a number of the knots in this chapter before deciding which ones best serve your needs. Some work better with smaller or larger cordage, some tie quicker and easier than others, and some are easier to untie. In some, the running ends lead out the side of the knot. In others, they lie along the standing parts. While some will be fun to tie, others may be too cumbersome. Whatever your preferences, the only way you will find out what you like is by trying out all these bends.

Overhand Bend

The Overhand Bend is quick to tie and is best used with small cordage like thread or string. It is secure, but makes a connection that is only half as strong as the material it is tied in.

 Place two ends of the cord or two cords next to each other, and use the double cord to tie an Overhand Knot.

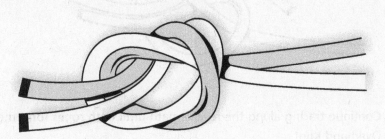

2 Tighten by pulling the standing parts in opposite directions.

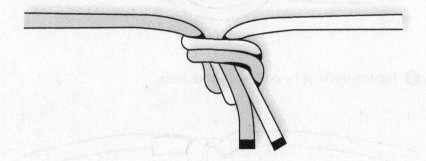

The Overhand Bend is also tied as a decorative way to combine a couple of loose ends. It can also be used to gather a large number of strands by just laying them all together and tying an Overhand Knot with all of them, though this use would be more like a binding knot in function.

Water Knot

The Water Knot is a strong knot that holds well with straps or flat webbing.

1 Tie an Overhand Knot in the end of one rope, then take a second rope and trace it through the knot in the opposite direction.

2 Continue tracing along the reverse path until both ropes form the Overhand Knot.

3 Tighten the knot by pulling on both ends.

The Water Knot is difficult to untie after being under strain. If you use flat material to tie this knot, be careful that the straps don't make a twist inside the knot, but that they lay down flat together, as in step 3.

Fisherman's Knot

Even though this is really a bend, it is known as the Fisherman's Knot, Englishman's Knot, and the Angler's Knot.

1 Lay two ropes parallel to each other and overlap each rope's running end around the other's standing part, making two Overhand Knots.

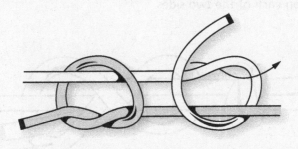

2 Tighten each Overhand by pulling on the two standing parts, so that the two ropes are held firmly together.

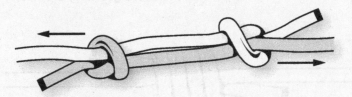

3 Pull the two ropes apart so that they form a circle, tightening each knot.

The Fisherman's Knot is difficult to untie and will work best when tied in small cordage. It is often chosen as a secure way to join two small lines of similar size.

Double Fisherman's Knot

The Double Fisherman's Knot is a bend tied in the same manner as the Fisherman's Knot, with two Double Overhand Knots in place of the regular ones.

 Lay two ropes parallel to each other and tie a Double Overhand Knot on each of the two sides.

2 Tighten up each Double Overhand Knot and pull the two ropes apart so that they form a circle, further tightening the knots.

This bend provides more security than the Fisherman's Knot, which you may need if you use very slippery lines or they differ in size a bit. If you need more security than that, you may consider using Triple Overhand Knots to fasten the two ropes. If more than a Triple is to be used in fishing line, it should be tied in the same manner as the Uni-Knot (see Chapter 11).

Surgeon's Bend

When the Surgeon's Knot is used to join two ropes, it can be called the Surgeon's Bend. (To learn how to tie a Surgeon's Knot, see Chapter 8.)

1 Start by passing one rope's running end over the other, making two passes.

2 Pull up the two running ends and pass one over the other, making a half knot.

When tightened down, this bend has a unique low-profile shape, which you can see in the following illustration of the Backing Up Bend. The Surgeon's Bend is secure in most materials, and relatively easy to untie.

Backing Up Bend

You can make a bend more secure by tying down the running ends. Backing Up is a good method for bends like the Surgeon's Bend, where running ends exit parallel to the standing parts.

▶ Tie down the running ends of a Surgeon's Bend with a Half Hitch (see Chapter 7) on each side.

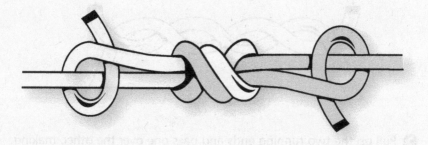

This extra tie-off can also be an Overhand Knot. When you make bends with climbing rope, you may also consider using Triple Overhand Knots as a backup—the extra tie-off will make the knot safer and will keep the running ends of the knot from waving around.

Sheet Bend

The Sheet Bend is widely used and is of the same structure as the Bowline Bend, but with the leads performing a different function. Consider the two ropes you need to join for this bend. If one of the ropes is larger, it should be used for the end that is folded over double.

 Take two pieces of rope. Take the rope on the left and make a loop, with the running end facing upward. Then, take the rope on the right and move the running end up between the loop and around the back of the other rope.

 Continue the tuck by moving the running end down and through the loop, under itself.

(continued)

Sheet Bend (continued)

3 Tighten the bend by pulling the slack out of the running end, and then pulling on the standing parts.

If the size difference between the two ropes is too much, or if the tying materials are slippery, the Double Sheet Bend may provide more security.

Slipped Sheet Bend

This bend is a modified version of the Sheet Bend. In this particular bend, the last tuck is made with a bight instead of a single running end.

 Follow step 1 for tying the Sheet Bend. As you move to step 2, double up the running end and use the bight to move through the loop and under itself.

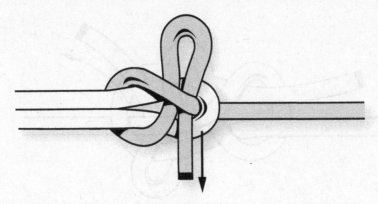

2 You can also tie a Slipped Bend by taking an extra turn around the knot before tucking the bight.

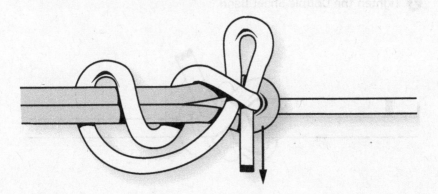

The Slipped Sheet Bend is at least as secure as the regular Sheet Bend, but with the added convenience of having quick release. The alternate slipknot shown in step 2 can be useful when there is a larger difference in rope sizes.

Double Sheet Bend

Another version of the Sheet Bend is the Double Sheet Bend, which you may prefer for use with two ropes that come in different sizes, or if you require a more secure bend.

 Start by making a Sheet Bend. Pass the running end around the knot again to tuck under its standing part a second time, making two wraps.

2 Tighten the Double Sheet Bend.

The Double Sheet Bend can be used to tie a rope to a clothlike material or the top of a sack, if the flat material is used as the end that is folded over.

Carrick Bend

The Carrick Bend is traditionally used on large ropes, such as ships' hawsers. When it has been under strain and perhaps wet, it is loosened by striking the outer bights of the knot with something blunt, like a wooden fid (an object like a marlinespike).

1 Lay down two ropes, one on the left and one on the right. Use the running end of the rope on the right to make a crossing turn. Take the other rope and move its running end in an over-and-under pattern through the other rope.

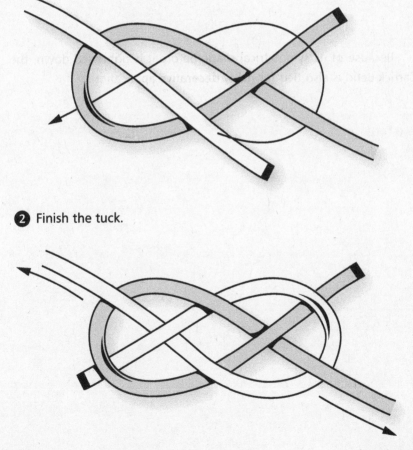

2 Finish the tuck.

(continued)

Carrick Bend (continued)

3 Pull on both standing ends, and take slack out with the running ends as well.

Because of its symmetrical shape before it is tightened down, the Carrick Bend is also tied for many decorative applications.

Hunter's Bend

Although most knots don't result in publicity, this knot did when Dr. Richard Hunter brought it to public attention, leading to the formation of the International Guild of Knot Tyers in 1982. Today, this knot is also called the Rigger's Bend.

 Start by placing the two ropes together, with the running ends facing opposite directions.

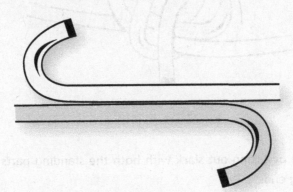

 Use both ropes to make a crossing turn.

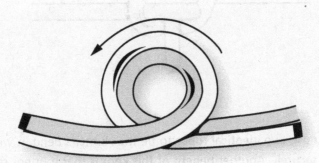

(continued)

Hunter's Bend (continued)

3 Tuck the running ends through the turn in opposite directions.

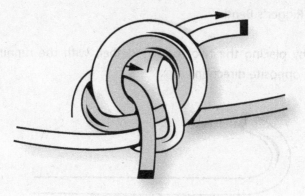

4 Tighten by taking out slack with both the standing parts and the running ends.

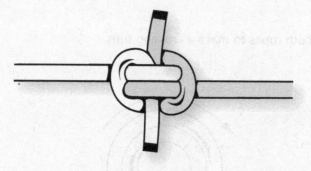

If you use two identical ropes to tie the Hunter's Bend, it will hold well and securely. Another benefit of this knot is that it unties readily.

Ashley's Bend

This knot is named after Clifford W. Ashley, who first introduced it in his book, *The Ashley Book of Knots.*

1 Take the first cord and make a crossing turn.

2 Take the second cord and use it to lace another crossing turn through the first cord.

(continued)

Ashley's Bend (continued)

3 Form the final tuck by bringing both running ends through the center together.

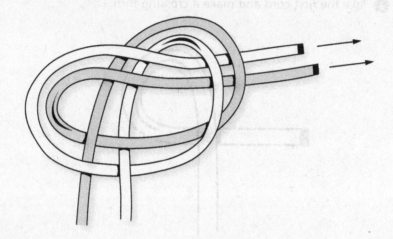

4 Tighten down the cord, forming Ashley's Bend.

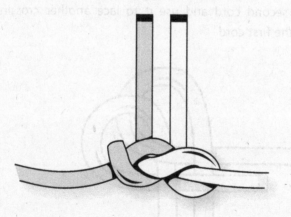

Ashley's Bend is very strong and secure when used to join similar ropes. It does not slip even when brought under severe shock loads, but can be untied easily when desired.

Zeppelin Bend

The Zeppelin Bend, also known as the Rosendahl Bend, is a good sailing bend to learn.

1 To start, place two ropes together and use one of the running ends to make a loop as shown in the illustration.

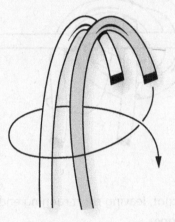

2 Next, separate the standing parts, moving one of them (the one at the end of the rope that did not form the loop) under the looped running end and over the other running end.

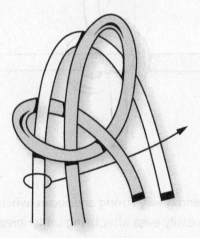

(continued)

Zeppelin Bend (continued)

3 Use the same rope's running end to make the final tuck.

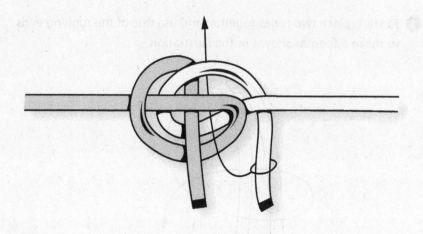

4 Tighten down the knot, leaving short running ends to stick out perpendicular to the ropes.

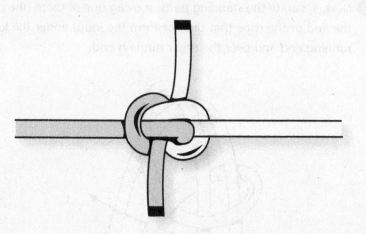

The Zeppelin Bend is very strong and secure when used to join similar ropes. It unties easily even after being under great strain.

Butterfly Bend

Also called the Straight Bend, this knot has the same form as the Butterfly Loop (see Chapter 6), and can even be tied the same way if the ends are attached.

 Place two ropes side by side—one on the right and one on the left—and cross the running ends, forming loops.

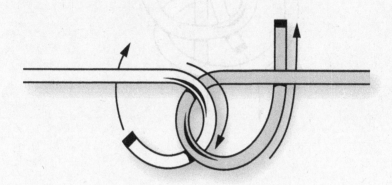

2 Use the right-side cord's running end to make a second loop.

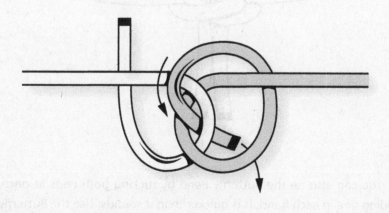

(continued)

Butterfly Bend (continued)

3 Use the left-side cord's running end to make its second loop as well.

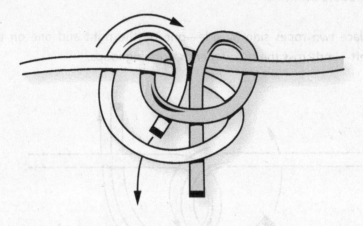

4 Tighten down the knot by pulling apart the two standing parts and tugging down the running ends.

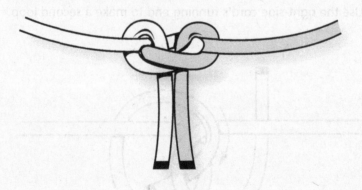

You can also tie the Butterfly Bend by tucking both ends at once, holding one in each hand. It is quicker than it sounds. Use the Butterfly Bend to tie similar materials. It is strong, secure, and unties easily.

Interlocking Overhand Bends

Each of the previous four bends consists of Interlocking Overhand Knots. Although each of these knots can be tied without reference to their overhand structures, they are illustrated here for the sake of the completeness of these very superb bends. As you can see in the following illustration, an Overhand Knot has three internal openings that can interlock with other knots. Making an Overhand Knot at the end of one rope, and then interlacing another Overhand through it can tie any of these bends.

1 A right-handed overhand knot

2 Hunter's Bend

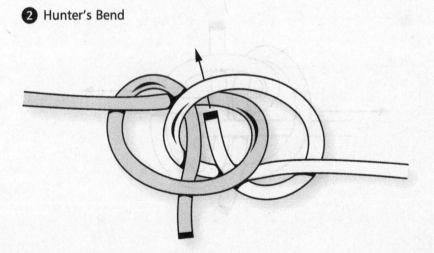

(continued)

Interlocking Overhand Bends
(continued)

3 Ashley's Bend

4 Zeppelin Bend

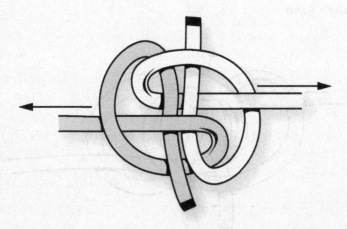

⑤ Butterfly Bend

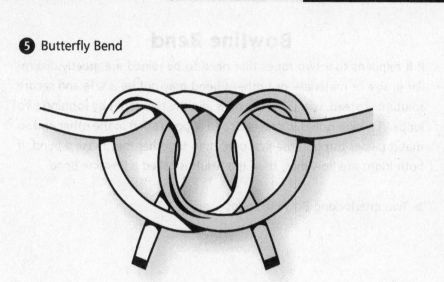

Can you see the Interlocking Overhand Knots in each one of these bends?

Bowline Bend

If it happens that two ropes that need to be joined are greatly dissimilar in size or material—or both—a bend may not be a safe and secure solution. Instead, what you can do is join the two ropes by forming two loops. If a loop is tied in one end, and a loop is tied in the other end so that it passes through the first one, then together they make a bend. If both loops are Bowlines, then the result is called a Bowline Bend.

▶ Two interlocking Bowline Loops

Bends are a basic and useful knotting concept that is both fun to try and important to use correctly and safely. When summing up what you have learned from this chapter, you should have a fair idea of which knots you would find useful, and you should practice and remember them so that you can use them correctly and safely.

6

Tying Loops

A ROPE WITH A LOOP TIED IN IT is a completely different tool than one without a loop. The majority of tasks you will ever do with rope or string can be done or aided by tying a loop in it.

What's the Use for Loops?

As the most versatile knot you can tie, a loop can function in any category of knot, including a stopper knot, hitch, part of a bend, and even as binding or decoration. A loop can be used as a hitch either by tying and then passing the loop over the end of an object, or by first passing the end around an object and then tying. Two interlocking loops can be used to fasten one rope to another, thereby making a reliable bend.

Loops by Type

There are many different loop knots to choose from. You can tie a loop at the end of a rope or in the middle. It can slide like a noose or be locked in place, or even have multiple turns.

A locked fixed loop does not slide and keeps its size when strain is placed on it. Once a locked loop is tied, it can be thrown over a peg or hook to secure the rope, and then lifted off and used again. If tied for a handhold or around your waist, it will not close down on you. The Bowline Loop is probably the most well known of this form. Some locked loops are made by splicing a three-stranded rope and using the strands to tie the loop.

When you need more than one loop, you can tie a knot with multiple loops. Complexly shaped objects can be hoisted without tilting, and a single rope can be fastened to multiple anchor points. Loops can even be different sizes. If you need a large number of custom-sized loops for hoisting or binding, you can start with a small fixed loop with a large running end left over. Repeatedly make your loops with the running end, passing it through the locked loop each time, tying off the last one.

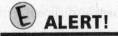 **ALERT!**

The Hangman's Noose is a popular knot but should never be toyed with. Children may try to re-enact how they see them used in TV Westerns, with tragic results.

You may need a loop that is adjustable in size. Sliding loops, also called nooses or slip loops, fill this purpose. Fishermen often want a loop that will hold its shape until just enough pressure is put on it, causing it to pull down with a jerk that sets a hook in a fish. Sometimes you just want your loop to fit something snugly, but need to tie it ahead of time. If you have a fixed loop and need to make it larger, you can just pull a bight of the standing part through the loop, giving you as large of a loop as needed. An example of this is the Running Bowline.

There is a world of loop knots to choose from, and even if you prefer to remember just one locked loop, you can make a sliding loop or a multiple loop from it. Loop knots are rewarding to learn and tie, and rope becomes quite a diverse tool when you learn them.

Overhand Loop

The Overhand Loop is a very common way of tying a loop. It's quick to tie and is especially useful with very small cordage like thread or string. It is difficult to untie after being under strain, so it is usually used when it is not meant to be untied.

1 Begin by folding over the running end to make a bight.

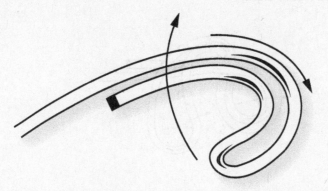

2 Tie the bight in an Overhand Knot, forming the Overhand Loop.

Note that the Overhand Loop can be tied near the running end or in the bight. If a Double Overhand is tied instead of a single one, it makes an excellent loop for string or fishing line.

Figure Eight Loop

The Figure Eight Loop is popular with climbers due to its distinctive look when tightened, which helps to determine whether it is tied correctly. For a high level of security, the running end can be secured to the standing part with a Triple Overhand Knot.

 Begin by folding over the running end to make a bight, and use it to form a Figure Eight.

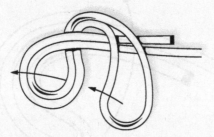

2 As you tighten the knot, the bight will form the loop.

Strong and secure, the Figure Eight Loop can also be tied around an object by making a regular Figure Eight Knot (see Chapter 4), leaving enough running end to bring around the object and then back to trace through the Figure Eight toward the standing part.

Bowline Loop

Commonly referred to as the "Bowline," this loop knot has been in such widespread use that it is also referred to as the "king of knots." It is still in much use today, and with a little caution can be used in the newer synthetic materials.

 Make a crossing turn.

 Bring the running end up through it, and then behind the standing part.

(continued)

Bowline Loop (continued)

3 Twist the running turn all the way around the standing part and back down through the crossing turn.

4 Take out all the slack to make the loop secure. As you tighten the knot, make sure you pull on all the leads.

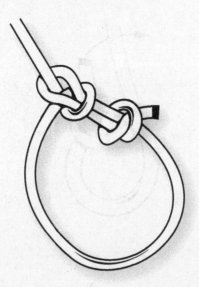

You can also tie the Bowline Loop with an extra hitch, especially if you want to increase security.

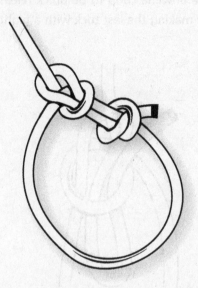

There's another way of tying the Bowline—by laying the running end down across the standing end. It's a quicker start, and you can tie the loop one-handed.

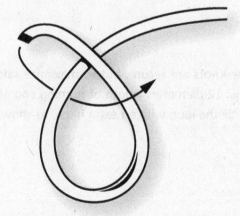

(continued)

Bowline Loop (continued)

If you want the Bowline Loop to be quick release, try the Slipped Bowline instead by making the last tuck with a bight.

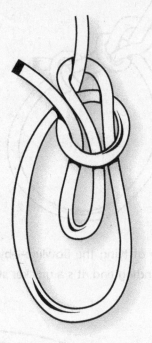

The Bowline Knots are secure, but to maximize safety, make sure you leave at least 12 diameters length of running end after the knot is tightened, and tie the loop with an extra hitch, as shown in step 5.

Double Bowline

The Double Bowline is similar to the Bowline Loop, but it's started with a double crossing turn.

1 Start with a double crossing turn.

2 Finish the knot just like a regular Bowline.

Also called the Round Turn Bowline, this version can provide for more security, especially if the rope used is very slippery.

Butterfly Loop

Also called the Alpine Butterfly, this loop is strong, secure, and easily untied after being put under strain. It's a great loop for use anywhere along a rope, and holds well even with strain put on both standing parts.

1 Twist the rope twice to make two adjacent crossing turns.

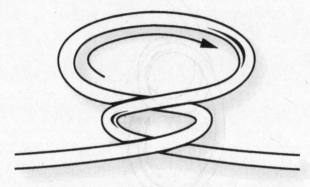

2 Pull down the outer turn.

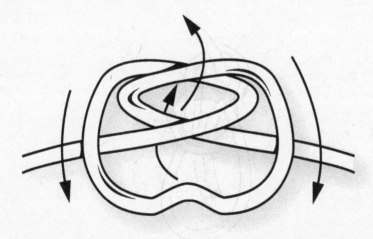

3 Bring the middle of the loop up through the center of the other crossing turn.

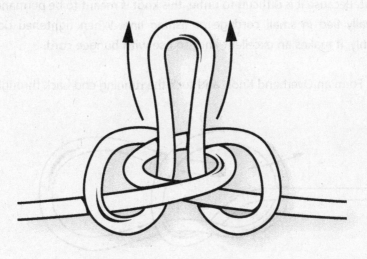

To tighten the loop, pull on all the leads. As you can see, the Butterfly Loop ties very quickly with just a little practice.

Angler's Loop

Both strong and secure, the Angler's Loop is a great general-purpose knot. Because it is difficult to untie, this knot is meant to be permanent, usually tied in small cordage or fishing line. When tightened down evenly, it makes an excellent knot to use with bungee cord.

1 Form an Overhand Knot, and tuck the running end back through it.

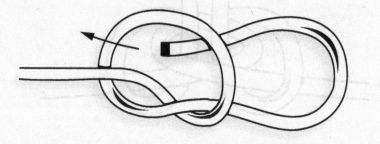

2 Trace the running end behind and around the standing part, and back through the knot.

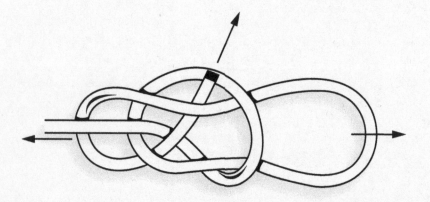

3 Tighten down the knot by pulling on all leads.

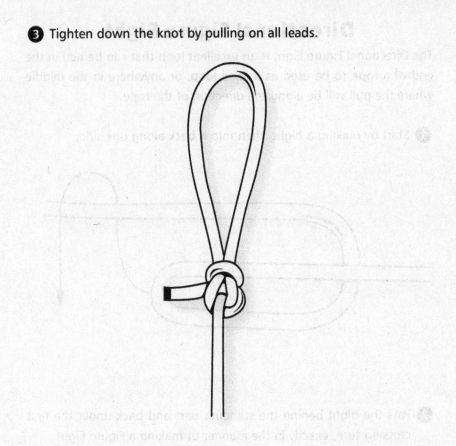

To tie the knot more quickly, note that tying a slipknot is a quick way to finish the first step.

Directional Figure Eight

The Directional Figure Eight is an excellent loop that can be tied in the end of a rope to be used as a fixed loop, or anywhere in the middle where the pull will be along the direction of the rope.

1 Start by making a bight, then fold it back along one side.

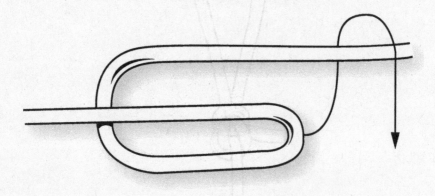

2 Pass the bight behind the standing part and back under the first crossing turn, exactly in the manner of making a Figure Eight.

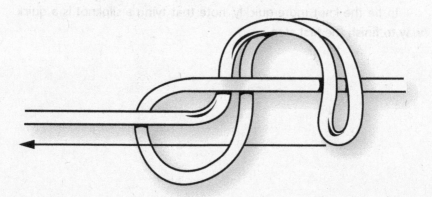

3 As you tighten the knot, the final loop will lay in the direction that strain will be placed on it.

The Directional Figure Eight can be tied so that the loop points right or left. The steps illustrated here result in a left-pointing loop. To tie a right-pointing one, start the first tuck in the opposite direction. A good rule of thumb to remember is that you start the first tuck in the opposite direction from which you want the loop to lay.

Honda Knot

Also called the Lariat Knot and the Bowstring Knot, this knot can be used to make an especially small loop because it is circular instead of oval, like most loops.

 Tie an Overhand Knot, then lead the running end back through it, finishing with another Overhand Knot at the tip. Then tighten down the first Overhand Knot. The second Overhand locks the loop.

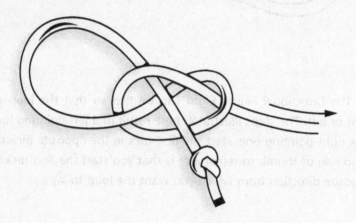

 If a running loop is desired, the Honda Knot itself can be tied around its standing part.

Running loop

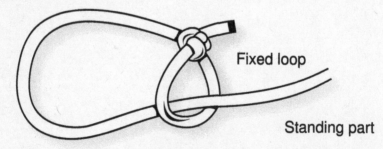

Fixed loop

Standing part

As you pass the running end through the Overhand Knot in step 1, it helps to remember that Overhand Knots have three openings. To be tied correctly, you must lead the running end through the opening closest to the loop, and take care that it stays in this part when tightening. If the lead slips into the middle part, the knot will not be secure.

The Honda Knot makes a good low-friction running loop. It is used to make a lariat, which is a running loop also known as a lasso. This knot has been used to tie off bowstrings because the size of the loop can be adjusted by changing the place of the Overhand Knot on the tip.

It's worth noting that the Honda Knot is tied in the same manner as the Guy Line Hitch (see Chapter 7). It is how they are used that makes them different. The Honda Knot is used when a locking loop is desired, and the Guy Line Hitch is used when the size of the loop will need to be decreased one or more times, thereby shortening the line it is tying off. If needed, however, the Honda Knot can be adjusted in size by changing the place on the locking overhand knot. This adjustability is why the Honda Knot has been used to attach bowstrings.

Eye Splice

Before you begin, you need to splice the running end. Unlay several inches of a three-strand rope, and tape or bind the area to keep the rope from unlaying further. The tucks start in a staggered order and proceed in an over-and-under pattern, just as when tying the Back Splice (see Chapter 4).

1 Make the first tuck by inserting the first unlaid strand through the intact strands of the rope.

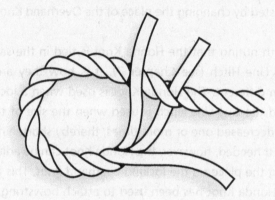

2 Start the next tuck by inserting the next unlaid strand through the same intact section of the rope, but this time tucking over and under.

Turn over the rope, and start the third tuck under the remaining strand.

 Continue tucks in an over-and-under pattern.

An Eye Splice is used to make a permanent loop in three-strand rope. It retains all of the strength of the rope, making it stronger than a regular loop knot. It is sometimes tied tightly around a protective thimble to protect the inside of the loop from abrasion. Each strand is usually tucked three times for natural fiber ropes, and up to five is sometimes used for more slippery synthetics. Sometimes the strands are thinned out after each level of tucks to taper the splice.

Portuguese Bowline

Before you start practicing this knot, review the steps for tying the regular Bowline Loop. Once you learn the Bowline, this knot is quick and easy to remember.

1 Start as you would to tie a regular Bowline, then use the running end to make a second loop.

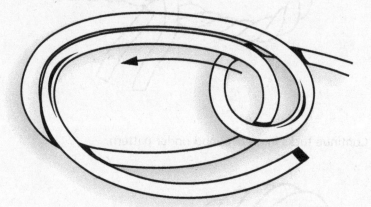

2 Continue the same as you would with a Bowline.

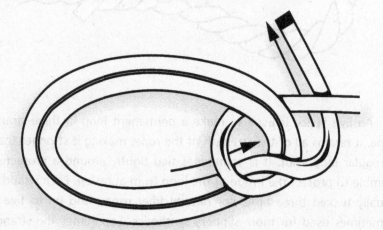

3 Finish by making the final tuck.

With the Portuguese Bowline, you'll have two loops that can be adjusted in relative size after the loop is tied, but the strain on both must be equal.

Triple Figure Eight

This loop is similar to the Figure Eight Loop, demonstrated earlier in this chapter. To start, you'll need to fold over the end of the rope, forming a long bight.

1 Use the doubled-up rope to start tying a Figure Eight Loop.

2 Pull through a bight of the doubled line.

Take the loop end and wrap it around the top, and then tuck it back down with the other loops.

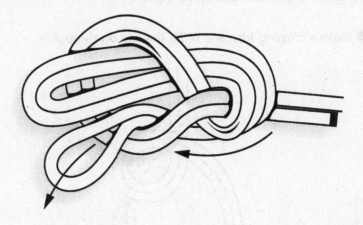

It will take a little practice to get a feel for how much line to use. Each of the three loops can be made a different size. Climbers use this knot to belay or fasten a line to three anchor points.

Bowline in the Bight

This knot is similar to the regular Bowline, except that you start out by folding the end of the rope into a bight.

1 Make a crossing turn and bring the end up through it.

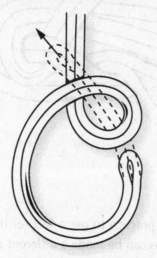

2 Open up the end loop and bring it down and under the two loops.

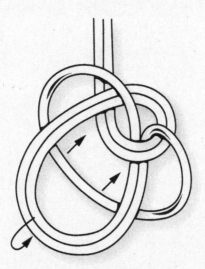

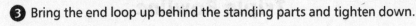

3 Bring the end loop up behind the standing parts and tighten down.

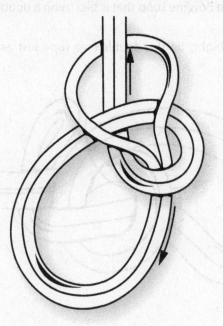

The Bowline in the Bight is quick, fun to tie, and makes a nice double loop. If tied near the end of a rope, the running end can be secured to the standing part with yet another Bowline. Just make a crossing turn in the standing part and bring the running end up through it, around the standing part, and back down through the crossing turn just like in a Bowline. This can be done with any knot where the running end comes out of the knot parallel to the standing part.

Triple Bowline

Another version of the Bowline Loop that is tied using a doubled-up rope.

 Starting with a bight, tie the doubled-up rope just as you would the Bowline.

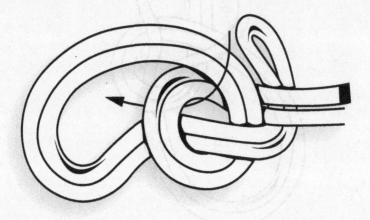

 Finish by tightening.

This loop knot is also good for fastening to multiple anchor points. It is easy to remember, and with a little practice you can make each of the loops different sizes.

Triple Crown Loop

The Triple Crown Loop Knot is much easier to learn if you have tied the Crown Knot found in Chapter 4, the chapter on stopper knots.

 Start with a bight, separate the end into two bights, and lay the standing part over one of them, making the first part of the crown.

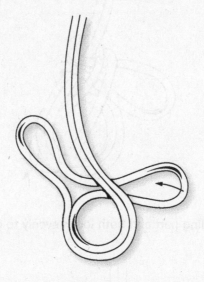

2 Fold the right side of the loop over the standing part.

(continued)

Triple Crown Loop (continued)

❸ Fold the left side of the loop over the right one and through the crossing turn.

❹ Pull the standing part and both loops evenly to get the final form.

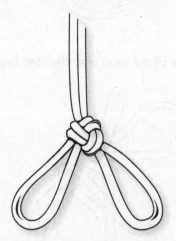

Strong and secure, the two loops of the Triple Crown Loop Knot can take strain independently. If the knot is tied close to the end, tie off the shorter standing part to the longer one with a knot of your choice—it will make the knot more secure. After tying the Triple Crown Loop, you can turn it over and crown it again if you like.

Slip Noose

A simple and quick-to-tie noose, the Slip Noose also serves as the start of the Oysterman's Stopper Knot.

1 After making a crossing turn, pull a bight from the standing end through it to make a noose of the desired size.

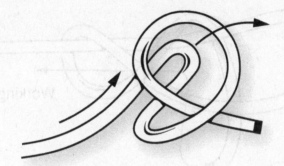

2 Tighten the noose.

A variation on this knot is the Slipped Noose (see Chapter 4), which occurs when the running end is tucked back along itself, such that it is now a bight leading from the knot instead of just the running end.

Double Overhand Noose

Also called the Poacher's Noose, the Poacher's Knot, and the Strangle Snare, this knot is a very good general-purpose noose to learn.

1 Tie a Double Overhand Knot with the running end over the standing part.

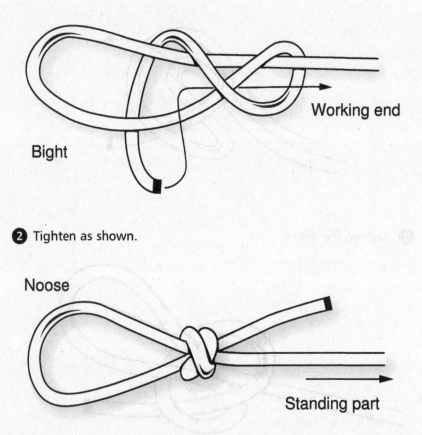

Working end

Bight

2 Tighten as shown.

Noose

Standing part

Because the Double Overhand Knot can hold tension when tightened down, the loop opening will not close down until it is pulled on, which helps to explain its nefarious past with poachers. Knots that make use of the Double Overhand structure remain very useful today due to their high security even when tied with slippery synthetic cordage. The Triple Overhand version of this knot is even more secure.

Running Bowline

You can tie a Running Bowline by tying a Bowline around its own standing part or by tying a Bowline the usual way, and then pulling a bight of the standing part through the loop.

1 Tie the Running Bowline by tying a Bowline around the standing part.

2 The result: Running Bowline.

If you make a fixed-loop knot like the Bowline or any other fixed-loop knot, and decide the loop part is not big enough, just turn it into a running loop knot and have the loop as big as you need it. Because the fixed loop part does not lock onto or grip the standing part, the noose will slide open easily even if great tension is placed on the sliding loop.

Hangman's Noose

This noose is also called Jack Ketch's Knot, named after a well-known hangman. It handles shock loads, and is also a handy way to store rope.

1 Fold the running end back along the standing part, and fold the new running end back on itself. Wrap the running end around the standing part, moving from bottom to top.

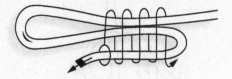

2 Tuck the running end through the top bight.

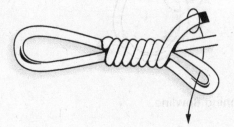

3 Put tension on the knot by pulling on the bottom loop.

The Hangman's Noose is the last loop in this chapter. Go back and review the chapter with the idea that some loops are locked and some slid. Your new understanding of the sliding loop will apply well to the next chapter on hitches.

7

Making Hitches

WHEN YOU NEED TO ATTACH A ROPE TO AN OBJECT, the knot for this job is called a "hitch." This is a common use for rope and you will find a variety of hitches in this chapter that will do a good job.

Attaching Rope to an Object

Hitches allow you to secure a rope to rings, rails, posts, hooks, other ropes, and other objects. Sometimes they are tied by forming the knot directly around the object, and sometimes by bringing the rope around the object and tying the running end to the standing part. If the shape of the object allows it, you can tie the hitch (or a loop) first, and then place it around the object. Some hitches, like the Rolling Hitch or Icicle Hitch, provide a friction grip to prevent them from sliding when strain is along the direction of the pole, rail, or rope.

You may want tension to remain in the rope after the hitch is tied. If you are frustrated by a little slack going into the rope as the hitch is tightened, you will find that making an extra wrap around the object, called "making a round turn," will help hold tension as the knot is tied. An example of this is the Round Turn and Two Half Hitches. Another option is to tie a hitch that allows you to take out slack repeatedly without untying the hitch itself, as with the Guy Line Hitch. Tying ropes without slack in them is useful for many applications, like when you need to secure cargo.

Most hitches are tied by using Half Hitches (see page 132) in various combinations. When using more than one, Half Hitches can have a left or right orientation, and many hitches are tied by combining just two Half Hitches. Some hitches that seem different from each other are in fact made with the same exact combination of Half Hitches—the only difference may be that in one case, the hitch is tied directly onto an object, and in the other, it is tied around the standing part. An example is the difference between the Clove Hitch and the Round Turn and Two Half Hitches.

Ⓔ ESSENTIAL

Rope bound tightly will protect cargo from shifting, but it can also damage it. Pulling a rope too tight, especially with a leveraged hitch like the Trucker's Hitch, will result in a crushing force that can crack a canoe or collapse a container. Rope can leave indentations in hardwood furniture. Use padding where the rope comes in contact with wood.

Leveraged Hitches and Slings

Some hitches allow you to put up to three times more strain on the rope than you are applying to tighten it. A Trucker's Hitch pulls on the rope as if you were using a pair of pulleys, allowing you to make pulling tackle from a length of rope. The magnification factor at any point is determined by how many ropes under equal tension are connected to it. Don't get confused by trying to think about which direction the rope is pulling. It helps to consider that a rope can only pull, not push.

Some hitches attach rope for pulling or hoisting large objects. The Timber Hitch is used on logs. The Barrel Sling can be used to hoist a barrel while holding it upright, and the Barrel Hitch is a sling that is tied like a Cow Hitch around an object. Its weight keeps the hitch snug.

It is rewarding to tie off a rope with the needed tension, and even be able to adjust it. Fastening ropes to objects can help with many jobs, and even more can be done when combined with other types of knots.

ⒺQUESTION?

How can I tie off something and make sure it stays secure?
In the Great Age of Sail, a hitch, or almost any knot for that matter, was not considered permanent unless the running end was seized. This binds the running end to the standing part, leaving no chance that the knot will come untied. How to seize a line is covered in Chapter 12.

Half Hitch

There are two basic ways of making a Half Hitch. It can be tied off with a running end, or it can be tied off with a bight, which makes it a Slipped Half Hitch.

 Bring the running end around the ring and then around its standing part. Then, tuck the end inside the crossing turn, next to the ring.

2 Another option is to make a last tuck with a bight, making it a Slipped Half Hitch.

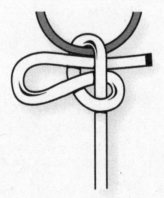

The Half Hitch makes a very quick and temporary tie off. It is also tied as the first step of other more secure hitches. The slipped version unties completely with just one pull.

Clove Hitch

This hitch ties quickly, but should not be considered a permanent connection or be used for safety or heavy loads.

1 Pass the running end around the object, cross over the standing part, and then pass the running end around the object again; then tuck it under the last crossing.

2 Tighten the knot around the object. Because the Clove Hitch can be tied in the bight, you can use any section of the rope to make the hitch that slides over posts.

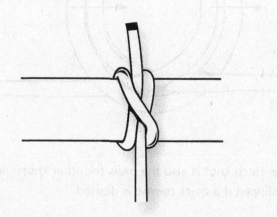

(continued)

Clove Hitch (continued)

3 Make two crossing turns and pass one in front of the other.

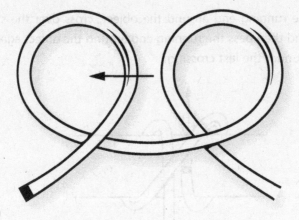

4 Place the formed double loop around the object to form the Clove Hitch.

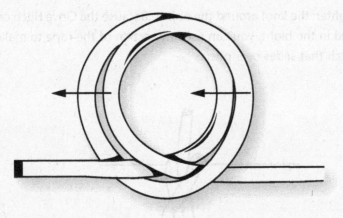

The Clove Hitch knot is also the basis for other knots, and the last tuck can be slipped if a quick release is desired.

Round Turn and Two Half Hitches

The instructions for tying the Round Turn and Two Half Hitches are built right into the name. It can also be thought of as tying a Clove Hitch around its own standing part.

 Use the running end to make a round turn over the object.

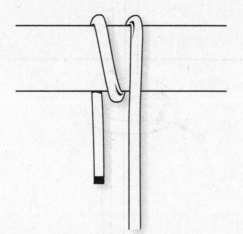

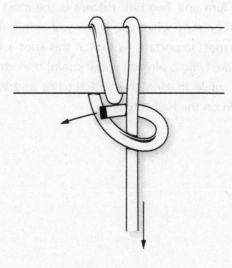 Tie a Half Hitch around the standing part.

(continued)

Round Turn and Two Half Hitches
(continued)

3 Next, tie a second Half Hitch.

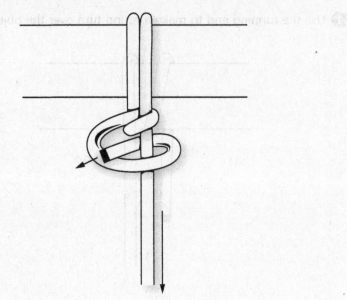

The Round Turn and Two Half Hitches is the most common hitch used for tying off a rope when you know you won't need to adjust it after tying. The most important feature of this knot is the round turn. If the rope you are tying is already under strain, the extra turn will help hold against it while making the Half Hitches and will continue to reduce the strain on the Half Hitches.

Cow Hitch

Also called the Lark's Head, the Cow Hitch is used in decorative work. It is only considered secure if the tension is on both ends.

1 Start by making a double crossing turn over an object.

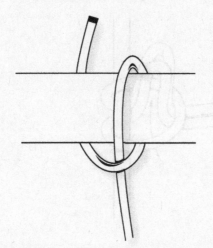

2 Finish like a regular Bowline—bring the running end down over the top and tuck it to exit parallel to the standing part.

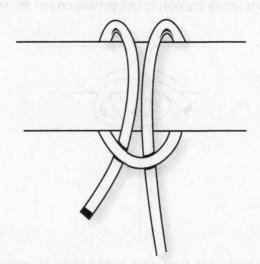

(continued)

Cow Hitch (continued)

3 Another way to tie a Cow Hitch is by first passing a bight behind and back over the object, and then pulling both ends all the way through the bight.

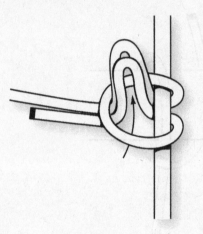

Another variation of the Cow Hitch is the Pedigree Cow Hitch—the difference is that you tuck the running end inside the turns for extra security. This hitch is secure enough to put tension on just the standing part.

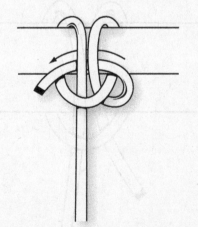

You can also tie the Cow Hitch in the bight by making opposing crossing turns and placing them together, leaving it ready to slide over an object.

Lobster Buoy Hitch

The Lobster Buoy Hitch is tied with just one turn around the object because using a round turn would take tension away from Half Hitches, reducing the advantage of trapping the running end.

▶ Bring the running end once around the object. Make two Half Hitches that form a Cow Hitch around the standing part, so that the running end is trapped against the object.

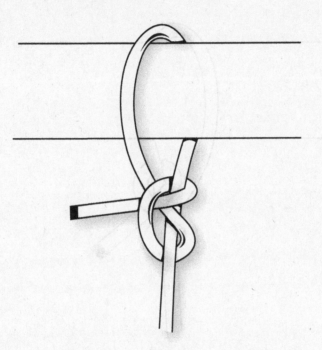

A useful feature of this hitch is that the running end is trapped, but not as tightly as in the Buntline Hitch.

Buntline Hitch

The name of the Buntline Hitch comes from its use on sailing ships as a hitch that would not shake free when both the rope and the sail (a bunt is the middle portion of a sail) it was tied to moved in the wind.

▶ Make one turn around the object, then make two Half Hitches (as shown). Note that the second Half Hitch is between the object and the first Half Hitch.

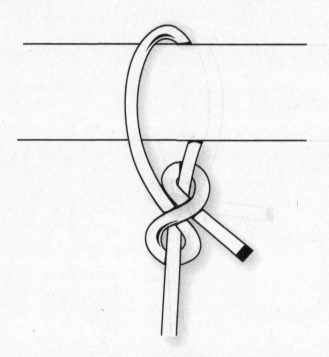

This hitch traps the running end very tightly. Learn this knot, and you will also know how to tie a common necktie knot, described in Chapter 11.

Anchor Hitch

Also called the Fisherman's Bend, even though it is a hitch and not a bend, the Anchor Hitch is commonly used to tie a rope to an anchor.

 Start with a round turn and pass a Half Hitch through both turns.

 Finish with a regular Half Hitch.

The Anchor Hitch stays secure when the rope drifts and the strength of pull changes. For larger boats, this hitch is relied on for repair more than a permanent connection. You can make the Anchor Hitch more secure by seizing the running end to the standing part (see Chapter 12 for information on seizing).

Timber Hitch

Just as its name suggests, the Timber Hitch is traditionally used to hoist or drag logs or poles.

1 Start by tying a Half Hitch.

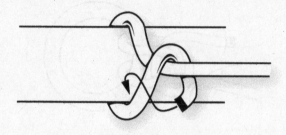

2 Continue making additional wraps, as shown.

As you can see, this hitch will work best if you place strain on it along the direction of the object the rope is hitched to—it will keep the knot tight.

Rolling Hitch

The Rolling Hitch can be tied to a pole or to another rope. It provides a friction grip to resist sliding if the pull is to the side with the round turn. It works best when the pole or rope it is being tied to is twice or more the diameter of the rope used to tie the hitch.

1 Start the hitch with a round turn.

2 Cross over and finish with a Half Hitch.

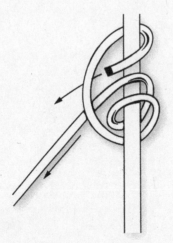

(continued)

Rolling Hitch (continued)

3 The knot should finish with both ends coming out together under the bight.

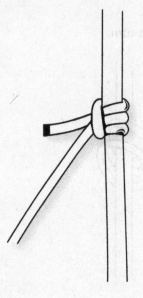

The Rolling Hitch is tied the same way as the Tautline Hitch, which is shown next.

Tautline Hitch

The Tautline Hitch is a very popular adjustable hitch and easy to remember if you know the Rolling Hitch. It allows you to adjust the size or tension in the rope after it is tied, making it very useful for securing cargo.

1 Bring the running end around the object to make a crossing turn, then back a distance and make two turns around the standing part.

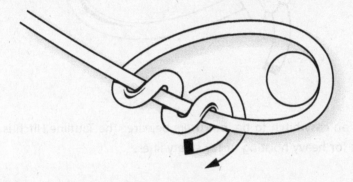

2 Finish the Rolling Hitch around the standing part.

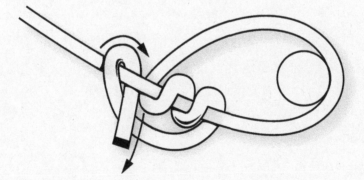

(continued)

Tautline Hitch (continued)

3 Tighten down the hitch.

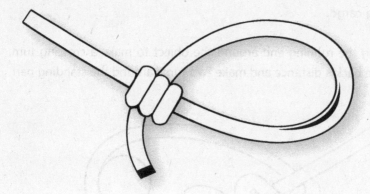

This is an easy hitch to tie, but users beware: The Tautline Hitch is not meant for heavy hoisting or for safety lines.

Guy Line Hitch

A "guy line" is a rope or wire used to hold a pole, antenna mast, or tent in place. There is generally more than one guy line, and when the Guy Line Hitch is used, the length and tension of each can quickly be adjusted.

1 Make an Overhand Knot some distance from the end, so that you leave enough running end to pass around the object and then back to the Overhand.

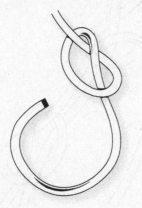

2 Pass the running end back through the bottom of the Overhand Knot.

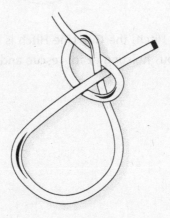

(continued)

Guy Line Hitch (continued)

Sometimes two Overhand Knots are tied next to each other in the standing part. The running end is passed through the first one to provide the grip and the second one to hold the end down.

3 Tie two Overhand Knots in the standing part, and tuck the running end into the second one.

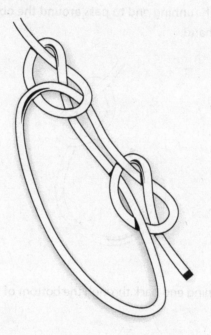

Like the Tautline Hitch, the Guy Line Hitch is meant for a support line and not for serious hoisting or for rescue and safety lines.

Marlinespike Hitch

The Marlinespike Hitch is named after a small metal bar used as a tying tool. It is tapered to a point at one end, which can be inserted into knots to work them loose, or into the strands of rope to aid with splicing.

 Twist the tip of the marlinespike so that the rope forms a crossing turn over it.

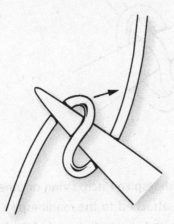

 Pull the bight across the standing part, forming what looks like an Overhand Knot.

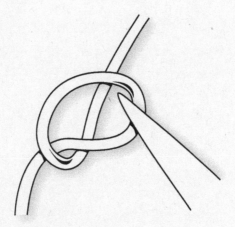

(continued)

Marlinespike Hitch (continued)

3 Lift the bight of the standing part up through the crossing turn.

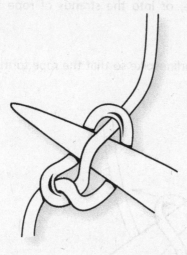

With the use of a Marlinespike Hitch, string or other small cordage can quickly and easily be attached to the marlinespike. By holding the marlinespike in your fist with the standing part of the hitch coming out between your two middle fingers, you can pull forcefully without the string cutting into your hand. A lashing or seizing can be made very tight this way.

Pile Hitch

The Pile Hitch is very quick and easy to tie, as long as you're working at the end of a stick or pole.

1 Pass a bight of rope around a post near the edge.

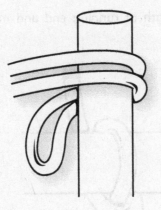

2 Open up the bight to pass it over the two standing parts and through the top of the post.

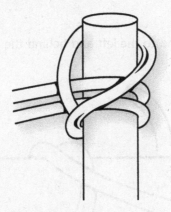

It helps to learn tying the Pile Hitch before going on to the Icicle Hitch (see the next knot), which is an extension of the Pole Hitch.

Icicle Hitch

John Smith of Surrey, England, first demonstrated the Icicle Hitch by using it to suspend his weight from a tapered wooden fid that was hanging point-down from the ceiling. Like finger cuffs, this hitch will shrink to grab strongly, then loosen easily when the strain is taken off.

 Start with a good length of running end and make a crossing shown here.

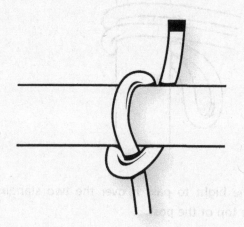

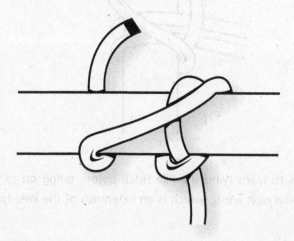 Cross the running end to the left and behind the pole.

Bring the running end around the pole, tucking it under the crossing. Complete four turns, tucking the end each time.

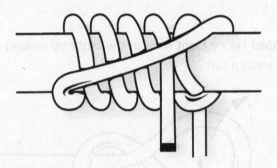

4 After the fourth turn, also tuck the running end under the first loop so that both ends exit together.

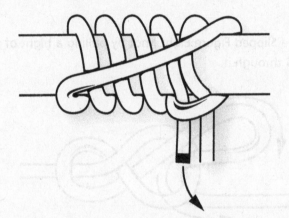

After you are finished, use the running end as the end that will take strain. This will allow the hitch to have its tenacious grip. Do this either by leaving a large excess of running end or by extending it by making a bend to another rope.

You can also tie the Icicle Hitch near the end of a pole, in a manner similar to the Pile Hitch. To see this, first tie it near a pole end with the method shown previously, then pull the bight over the end as if you were untying the Pile Hitch, and you will see the setup for this method. When checking to see if you have tied it correctly, keep in mind that this hitch is basically an extended Pile Hitch.

Trucker's Hitch

The Trucker's Hitch is tied with a Slipped Figure Eight Knot, shown in Chapter 4.

 Start a Slipped Figure Eight Knot in the bight by making an extra twist to a crossing turn.

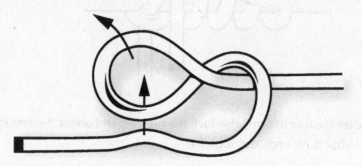

2 Finish the Slipped Figure Eight Knot by pulling a bight of the running end through it.

3 Treat the resulting loop as if it were a pulley by passing the running end around the anchor point and then back through the loop.

Bring the running end back up through the loop and pull it toward the anchor point to tighten the standing part.

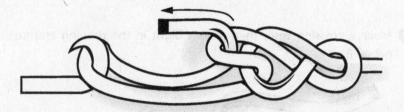

5 Secure the knot with two Half Hitches.

Make the loop as far from the anchor point as needed to take out slack in the standing part. Other loop knots can be used instead of the Slipped Figure Eight Knot, such as the Directional Figure Eight or the Butterfly Loop. The Slipped Figure Eight Knot is used most often, as it is quick to tie and untie, and has a strong lead that is not very damaging to rope.

Wagoner's Hitch

The Wagoner's Hitch is a leveraged hitch very similar to the Trucker's Hitch.
It needs tension on it to stay secure, and it comes undone with just a shake.

1 Make a crossing turn, then grab a bight in the running end just below it.

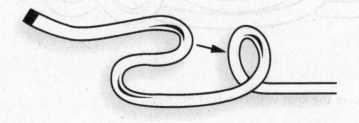

2 Pull the bight of the running end through the crossing turn. This forms a lower loop that the running end will pass through after it goes around an anchor point.

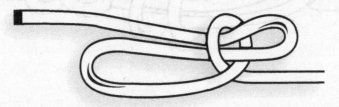

3 Pass the running end around the anchor and back up through the lower loop.

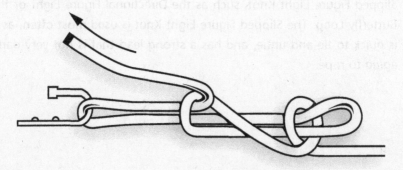

Barrel Sling

The Barrel Sling will hoist a barrel while keeping it upright.

❶ Stand the barrel upright on the middle of a short length of rope, and cross the ends together on top, making an Overhand Knot around the barrel.

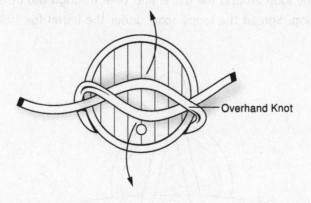

Overhand Knot

❷ Spread the crossed parts of the Overhand Knot over the sides of the barrel, then tie the ends together to serve as a hoisting sling. A Fisherman's Knot or Hunter's Bend will work well to complete a closed loop for hoisting.

Make sure that the sling is symmetrical on the barrel before lifting.

Barrel Hitch

This hitch is similar in form to a Cow Hitch. If a barrel or other short cylindrical object can be lifted on its side, the Barrel Hitch can do the job of hoisting it.

▶ Start with a strop or length of rope tied in a closed loop. Pass the end of the loop around the barrel and then through the other side of the loop. Spread the loops apart under the barrel for more stability.

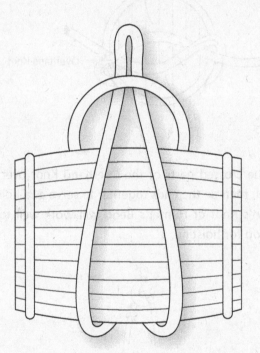

The more you work with hitches, the more you should have an idea of what they can do, and more importantly, what they can do for you. Fastening a rope to something is key to using rope for holding and moving objects, and it is best to learn more than one method. Also, the skills you obtain for fastening rope to objects will play an important part in how to use rope for bindings.

8

Knots That Bind

WITH A LITTLE KNOWLEDGE OF BINDING KNOTS, a small rope or stout piece of string becomes a multipurpose tool. Whether for decoration or emergency repairs, you will be glad you learned these basic binding knots.

Basic Applications

A binding knot can be used to grip and confine a single object. The most common example of a binding knot is the one you use to tie your shoes. Binding knots can also be used to combine and restrict a group of objects, like a bundle of firewood.

Ⓔ ESSENTIAL

Knots used for binding should generally not be used for something else, such as a bend or hitch. Binding knots like the Reef or Square Knot need to stay flat against a surface, and they lose stability when subjected to the uneven forces that are at play with bends or hitches.

Making temporary repairs is one of the applications where binding knots really show their worth. Using knots that can hold tension on a binding can be especially useful. The tremendous grip of the Boa Constrictor Knot can be used to secure a wooden pole that has cracked. A regular Constrictor Knot works like a hose clamp and can be slipped for quick release.

Tying Binding Knots

Binding knots can be tied in two different ways. One is to circle the object one or more times with a single piece of cord, and then tie the ends together. A Reef Knot or Butcher's Knot would be done this way. The other option is to circle the object two or more times, and then tuck and trap the ends under these turns. The Constrictor Knot binds this way, as does the Turk's Head (shown in Chapter 10).

 QUESTION?

How can I keep a binding tight while finishing the knot?
One way is to use the Constrictor Knot. Once you have tightened it, it is done! You can even tighten it more just by pulling on the leads.

When learning binding knots, it is as important to practice using them as it is to practice making them. Lashings and package tying can also be thought of as a form of binding; they are covered in the next chapter.

Reef Knot

Also called the Square Knot, this knot has been in common use for centuries for tying packages and bundles of all kinds. It is also used to tie bandages because it lies flat, making the dressing more effective and comfortable.

1 Pass one end over and around the other, making a Half Knot, just as if you were tying an Overhand Knot with two ends of the same piece.

First Working End

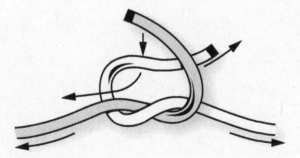

2 Tie a second Half Knot by tucking the right end over the left one.

(continued)

Reef Knot (continued)

3 Pull on both ends to tighten. Note that each end will exit next to its standing part.

Finished knot is symmetrical

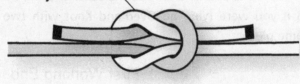

As you tie the Reef Knot, it may help you to say to yourself, "Left over right, right over left." To loosen the knot quickly, jerk one of the ends over the knot away from its own standing end, causing the knot to capsize. There are two common mistakes made with this knot. One is to make both Half Knots the same, making a very poor Granny Knot, and the other is to use this knot as a bend, which is not reliable.

Slipped and Double Slipped Reef Knots

Here are two other variations on tying a Reef Knot.

1 To make a Slipped Reef Knot, start by tying the Reef Knot, but tuck one of the ends with a bight.

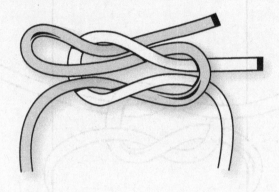

2 To make a Double Slipped Reef Knot, tie the second Half Knot with bights at both ends.

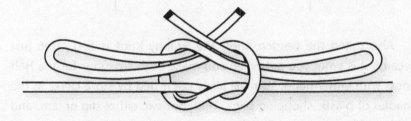

The Reef Knot is commonly slipped for ease of untying or for decoration. The Double Slipped Reef is commonly used to tie shoes and is tied with ribbon around packages to accentuate the decorative bows.

Granny Knot

The Granny Knot is a variation on the Reef Knot, except that the two Half Knots are the same.

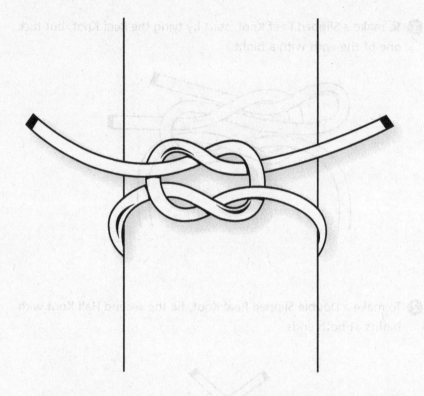

Also called the Garden Knot, the Granny Knot is tied often just because it is what you get when you make both crossings for the Half Knots with either hand. You will likely see it tied by store clerks in the handles of plastic shopping bags. This knot will either slip or jam, and can be difficult to untie. People often tie the double slipped version of this knot when attempting to tie a Double Slipped Reef in their shoelaces, which is evident when the knot's bows run up and down the length of the shoe instead of across.

Surgeon's Knot

Used by surgeons to tie off blood vessels, the Surgeon's Knot works well with small and slippery tying materials. Because the first crossing is double, it holds tension better than a Half Knot while completing the top half of the knot.

 Make the bottom half of the knot with two crossings instead of the single crossing of the Half Knot.

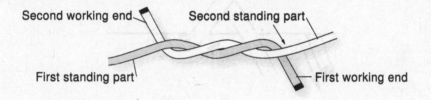

Second working end Second standing part

First standing part First working end

2 Finish the top half with a single crossing, as for the Reef Knot.

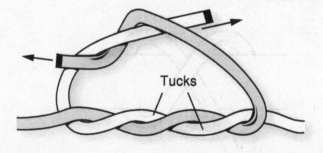

Tucks

If you wish, you can also tie the top half of the Surgeon's Knot with two crossings.

Constrictor Knot

Start this knot exactly as you would the Clove Hitch (Chapter 7). Only the last tuck is different, as shown in step 3.

 Pass the running end over and around the pole, crossing over the standing part, and behind the pole.

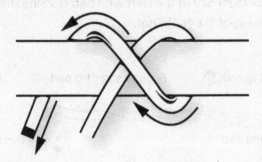

② Bring the running end from behind the pole and up over the standing part.

3 Tuck the end under the center X-shaped part of the knot. If you are able to place the Constrictor Knot at the end of the pole or another object, you can use the following method.

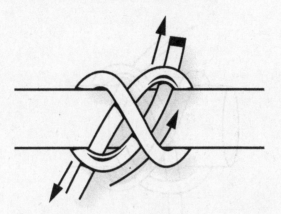

4 Make a single turn around the end of the pole, then pull down on the bottom part of the turn and twist it to make a crossing turn.

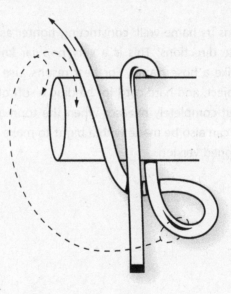

(continued)

Constrictor Knot (continued)

5 Pull the crossing turn over the standing part and the end of the pole.

This knot earns its name well, constricting tighter as the ends are pulled in opposite directions. This is a very popular knot because it functions much like a hose clamp. For best results, use soft cord for binding a hard object, and hard cord for binding a soft object. It is difficult to untie, but completely releases when the topmost crossing is cut. The last tuck can also be made with a bight to make a much more easily released slipped version.

Boa Constrictor

Also known as the Boa Knot, the Boa Constrictor forms an even more tenacious hold than the regular Constrictor Knot.

1 Begin by forming two crossing turns.

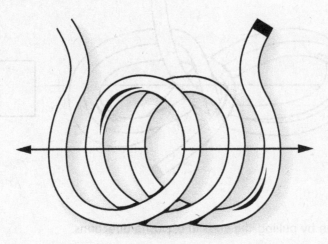

2 Overlap the crossing turns and twist one end over by a half turn.

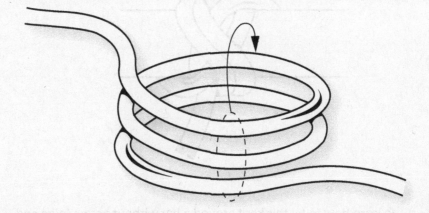

(continued)

Boa Constrictor (continued)

3 Place over the end of a pole, as shown. (The ends can be folded up to ease placement.)

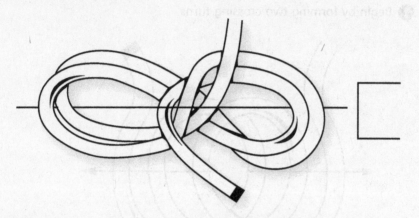

4 Tighten by pulling the ends in opposite directions.

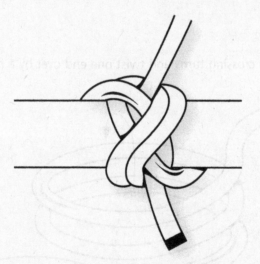

To learn how to tie this knot around a bar without access to an end, first tie it with this method, place it over a bar or pole end, then untie with just one end to see how the wraps and tucks are made.

Loop and Hitches

If you want to secure rope around an object, the Loop and Hitches method will make it easy. The following begins with a Bowline, but you can use another fixed loop (for instance, an Overhand Loop) instead.

 After tying the Bowline in one end, pass the other end around the bundle (or another object) and through the loop.

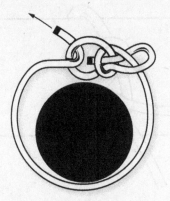

2 Pull away from the looped end to tighten the rope around the bundle, and finish with a couple of Half Hitches.

When the end is pulled back to tighten, the tension in the rope is double what you are pulling. For additional force, make a "loop in the bight" of the main loop, and pass the running end through it, as in a Trucker's Hitch. A second Trucker's Hitch made with the running end will magnify the pull even more.

Butcher's Knot

The Butcher's Knot is commonly used by butchers to secure joints of meat.

1 Tie a Figure Eight Knot (see Chapter 4) near the running end. Then, pass the standing part over and around the object, so that it comes back out through the bottom of the Figure Eight.

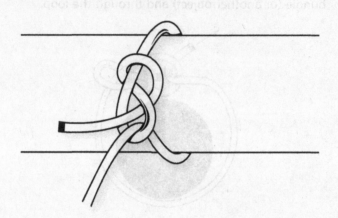

2 Make a Half Hitch with the standing part around the running end of the Figure Eight.

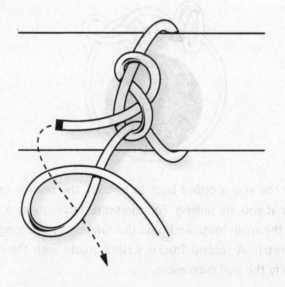

3 Finish the knot by tightening.

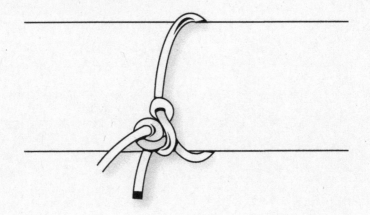

As you tighten the knot, hold tension on the running end of the Figure Eight Knot. This will aid in holding the wrap tight while making the final Half Hitch. The Butcher's Knot should not be considered a permanent binding, but you can make it more secure by adding an Overhand Knot to the running end of the Figure Eight Knot.

9

Knots for Lashing

FOR OUR ANCESTORS, a simple lashing meant the difference between swinging a sharp rock and swinging an ax. This skill remains important today, if not for axes, for lashing together poles and tying up packages and bundles.

Lashing Bundles

Wrapping and securing bundles is a form of lashing, so package ties (also called parcel ties) are included in this chapter. You can use lashing bundles to secure a single object, like a box or rolled-up sleeping bag. Or you can group a stack of items, like books or newspapers. The rope or string itself can serve as a handle to lift the object. String or small cordage is often used in place of wire to bundle items in industrial applications, because wire can do more damage to any machinery it gets caught in.

Ⓔ FACT

Until very recently, you could purchase parcel string at shipping supply stores, but not so much anymore. As quick and handy as parcel ties are, they have fallen out of favor because the string has a tendency to get caught in modern machinery used by shipping companies.

Lashing Poles

Lashing two or more poles together can be very useful for both construction and repair—to give more length or to make scaffolding, ladders, or makeshift furniture. Poles can be lashed parallel to each other or at right angles.

Ⓔ QUESTION?

How do I lash poles that are not exactly parallel or at right angles?
Position the poles parallel to each other and loosely tie a Sheer Lashing. Then the lashing will tighten as the poles are twisted open. You can also do this with three poles, and then open them up to make a tripod.

Key to making a pole lashing is the concept of the frapping turn. While the multiple wraps around two poles provide the structural strength that a lashing needs, the frapping constricts the wraps and creates the tension that holds them in place. If the poles are tied together parallel to each other as in the Sheer Lashing, the wraps must be loose enough to allow a couple of frapping turns to pass between them.

Sheer Lashing

Also called Round Lashing, this method will bind two poles parallel to each other.

1 Anchor the rope to one of the poles with a Clove Hitch (see Chapter 7).

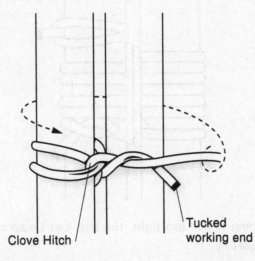

Clove Hitch

Tucked
working end

2 Wrap the rope around both poles with light and even tension, leaving enough space between them for the frapping turns. Continue making wraps until you cover a distance that's about twice the width of a single pole.

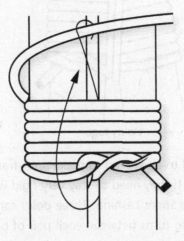

(continued)

Sheer Lashing (continued)

3 Make two frapping turns and finish with a Clove Hitch.

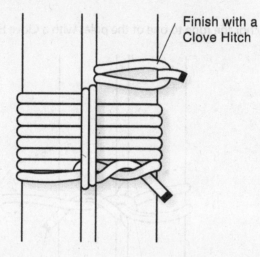

Finish with a
Clove Hitch

4 If the lashing is not too tight, the legs can be spread to use as "sheer" poles.

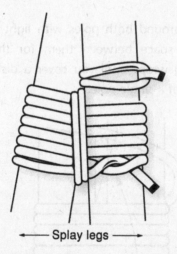

—— Splay legs ——

If the poles need to be spread to make an A-frame, make sure the tension is moderate. If they need to stay very rigid with each other, try using more than one Sheer Lashing. Three poles can be tied in similar fashion, with frapping turns between each pair of poles.

Transom Knot

The Transom Knot is a good way to tie two sticks perpendicular to each other if you want a lashing that is not bulky. The ends can be cut off close to the knot.

 Arrange the two sticks so that one is laid across the length of the other, and tie them together with a Double Overhand Noose Knot (see Chapter 6).

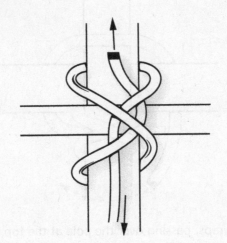

 Tighten the rope by pulling the ends in opposite directions.

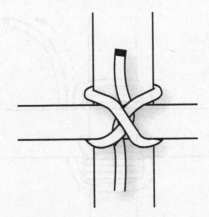

The top part of this knot has the same crossings as the Constrictor Knot, which is why this simple little knot grabs so well.

Square Lashing

If you are making scaffolding or other large square frames, Square Lashing is the method to use on the corners that meet at right angles.

1 Arrange two poles at a 90-degree angle to each other. Anchor one end with a Clove Hitch and start wraps, as shown.

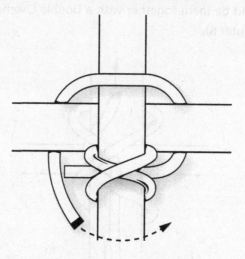

2 Make four wraps, passing over the pole at the top, and under the pole at the bottom, keeping each wrap tight.

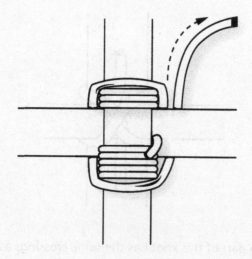

3 Make two frapping turns, staying in front of the back pole and behind the front pole, just as you would do with a Sheer Lashing.

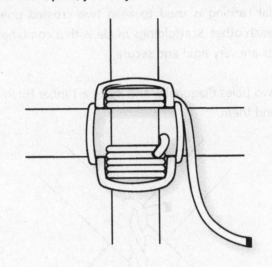

4 Tie off the remaining end with a Clove Hitch.

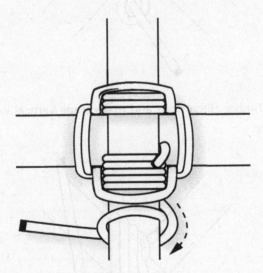

Note that no slack needs to be saved for the frapping turns, so keep tension on at all stages of this knot.

Diagonal Lashing

Whereas Square Lashing would be used to attach poles at right angles, the Diagonal Lashing is used to keep two crossed poles rigid with respect to each other. Scaffoldings made with a combination of these two lashings are very rigid and secure.

1 Cross two poles diagonally, and make a Timber Hitch (see Chapter 7) around them.

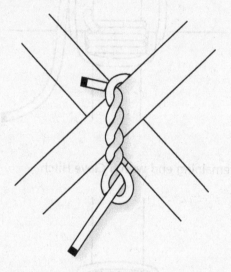

2 Pull the Timber Hitch tight and make three vertical wraps around the center.

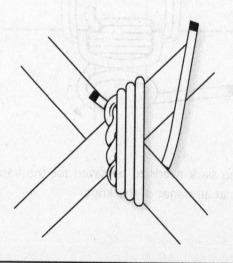

❸ Cross over and make three more wraps around the opposite diagonal.

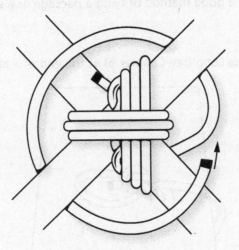

❹ Make two frapping turns, below the upper pole and above the lower pole, just as with the Sheer Lashing. Finish with a Clove Hitch (see Chapter 7).

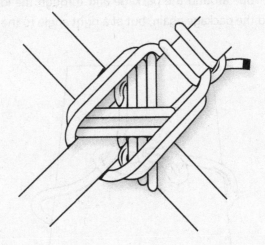

Parcel Tie

The Parcel Tie is a good method of tying a package or a stack of books or newspapers.

1 Tie a Bowline Loop (see Chapter 6) at the end of a length of rope.

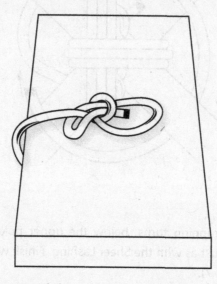

2 Pass the rope around the package and through the loop, then lead it around the package again, but at a right angle to the first crossing.

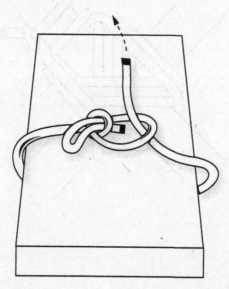

3 As you cross the length of rope with the running end underneath the package, maneuver it to tie a Crossing Knot (the illustration here is the view of the underside).

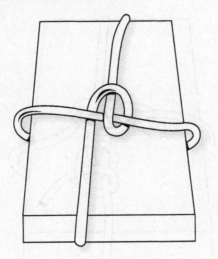

4 Next, bring the running end around to the front and pass it through loop again.

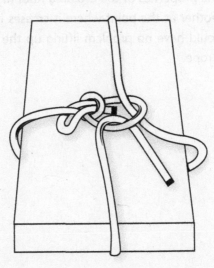

(continued)

Parcel Tie (continued)

5 Finish by securing the end with two Half Hitches.

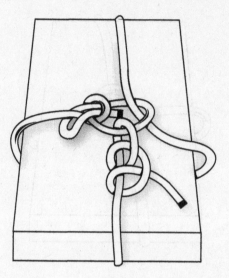

Thanks to the properties of the Crossing Knot (a knot made by one rope around another at the point where it crosses it, then continuing past it), you should have no problem lifting up the bundle by pulling on the knotted rope.

Marling

This type of lashing relies on Marling Hitches to hold the contents of a bundle firmly in place.

1 Start by securing the rope around the end of the bundle with a Timber Hitch (see Chapter 7). Lead the running end partway down the bundle, make another wrap, and tuck the running end over and under, as shown.

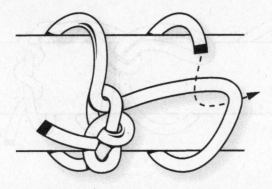

2 Continue with a few additional wraps along the length of the bundle. To secure the last Marling Hitch, tie one or two Half Hitches.

In forming each Marling Hitch, the running end is brought over and then under. If you tie each by going under then over, they form a series of Half Hitches, making a parcel tie called Single Hitches. Using Marling Hitches holds the bundle more securely, but takes longer to untie.

Chainstitch Lashing

Chainstitch Lashing holds well on bundles that are awkwardly shaped or that flex. You can also use it for decorative purposes.

1 Make a Timber Hitch at one end of the bundle (see Chapter 7). Fold a bight in the running end close to the Timber Hitch and then pull another bight through it after first passing it around the bundle.

2 Continue passing new bights around and through the previous bight. To finish, pull the entire running end through the last bight (instead of another bight) and secure with two Half Hitches.

Though it may look complicated, Chainstitch Lashing ties quickly once you get the knack.

10

Decorative Knotting

THOUGH THE WORD *DECORATIVE* SOMETIMES implies that little or no function is served, the craft of decorative knot tying generally combines both form and function. This chapter is a brief survey of decorative knots and their applications.

Tying Decorative Knots

You can do decorative knotting with both single and multiple strands. When using a single rope or cord, a set of wraps and tucks are made with just one end until you're finished. The Monkey's Fist (described in Chapter 4) is one example of this kind of knot. Multiple-strand knots often involve less for the knot tyer to remember than with single-strand knots. These decorative knots generally involve interweaving a set of cords in a repeating pattern to build up to the required size. The Matthew Walker Knot (also described in Chapter 4) is a favored decorative knot, sometimes tied in four or more strands.

There are a number of things that can aid your pursuit of the craft of decorative knot tying. A good general knowledge of knots is very useful. Many decorative knots are combinations of simple knots. The Constrictor Knot is commonly employed to control a group of strands, making them easier to hold in place. Pointed tools can help you pass cord ends through small openings and using pliers will help you pull them tight. And, of course, practice helps, because interwoven patterns always look nicer when they are even.

ⓔ QUESTION?

How do I get the decorative knots to come out more evenly?
With practice, you will get a feel for pulling evenly on all the strands. In the case of multistrand knots, slack needs to be taken out a little at a time, one strand at a time. For long single-strand knots, hold the shape of the knot during completion.

Uses for Decorative Knots

Some knots generally serve just one purpose, while others can serve many. Mat knots usually serve as a protective layer. When made with large enough rope, they can be used to make floor mats, or with smaller cord for drink coasters. Sennits, like the Crown Sennit described in this chapter, are best served as part of a handle of some kind, as in a key fob, bell pull, or light-switch pull. Coxcombing makes a covering for a long cylindrical object. It can act as abrasion resistance when tied around the loop part of an Eye Splice, or it can help improve grip when tied over a handrail.

The most versatile of all decorative knots is the Turk's Head. It can be employed as a protective covering, a binding, a hand-hold, or tied around the wrist or ankle as jewelry. It can stiffen weakened poles, gather a neckerchief, or stop a hitch from sliding. You can tie one as a napkin ring, shot glass base, or even flatten it out to make a mat.

Decorative knot tying can be as involved or as simple a craft as you want it to be. Chapter 14 gives suggestions for further study, or you can experiment on your own. Either way, the more you learn about general knotting the more you can do.

Three-Strand Braid

The most common use for this braid is for braiding hair. However, it's also a good way to tie three lengths of rope into a single braided rope for more strength.

 To start, you'll need three cords. The cords may simply be held together, or you can tie them together at the top. To start braiding, move the left cord to cross over middle cord.

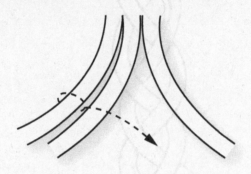

 Next, take the right cord and cross it over the new middle cord.

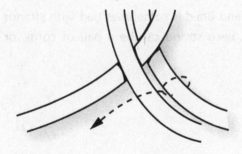

(continued)

Three-Strand Braid (continued)

3 Continue making crossovers, alternating sides until the braid is as long as you need it to be. Secure the ends, if necessary.

The Three-Strand Braid is sometimes tied with strands of different colors. Moreover, each strand can be a pair of cords, or a group of cords.

Ocean Plait Braid

Use the Ocean Plait Braid to make a floor or table mat. Old ropes may be retired to serve as material for these mats. To make an Ocean Plait mat, you'll need a longer length of rope than you think, especially if you plan to triple or quadruple the pattern to make the mat larger.

 Start by making a right-handed Overhand Bend and lay it on a flat surface with the ends of the rope pointed upward.

 Pull down both bights of the Overhand and twist each once to the left, forming two crossing turns. Pull the left crossing turn over to the right, and then pull the left side of the right crossing turn through the left crossing turn.

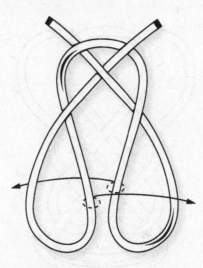

(continued)

Ocean Plait Braid (continued)

3 Bring down each end and weave it through the mat to give the finished over-and-under pattern.

4 The ends should be interweaved as shown.

It might take a little practice to keep the pattern symmetrical. As you weave the rope, check that the crossings always alternate over and under, never crossing under or over twice consecutively, unless of course the pattern is doubled. The ends can either be seized (see Chapter 12) or sewn in place.

Turk's Head

This knot is known as a three-lead four-bight Turk's Head because it makes three turns around the bar and each rim has four bights. It can be tied over the hand or around a cylindrical object. If tightened, the Turk's Head can serve as a binding. To use this knot in making a mat, widen one of the rims while pushing the other to the center, making the knot flat.

 Pass the running end twice around the bar, then over and under as shown by the arrow.

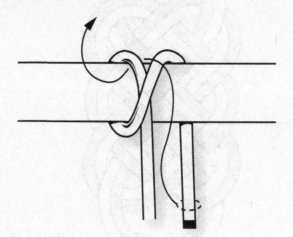

2 Flip the right crossing over the left one.

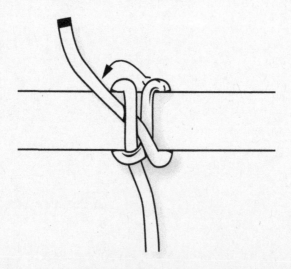

3 Thread the running end through the right crossing.

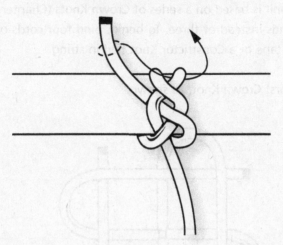

4 To double the knot, bring the running end around the back to the original start and follow the same pattern, staying next to the cord you are doubling without crossing over it.

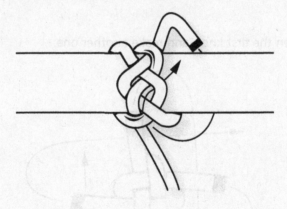

When you tie the Turk's Head, you are braiding in a circle, so it helps to rotate it toward you as you proceed.

Crown Sennit

The Crown Sennit is based on a series of Crown Knots (Chapter 4), but with four strands instead of three. To begin, bind four cords or ropes together, with tape or a Constrictor Knot tied in string.

1 Form the first Crown Knot, as shown.

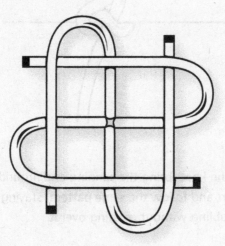

2 Tighten the first knot, and make another one.

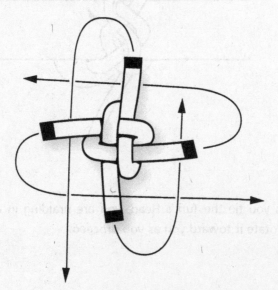

3 Tighten the second knot on top of the first one and continue tying Crown Knots, one on top of the other.

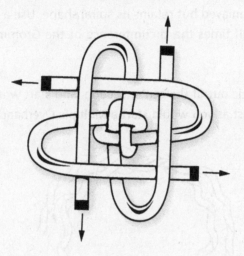

4 Repeat the Crown Knots until the sennit reaches desired length.

If you alternate the direction of each successive Crown Knot, the result will be a Square Crown Sennit. Other variations include using strands of different color or using eight cords instead of four. Crown Sennits may be used as decorative handles for key rings, bell clappers, and other objects.

Rope Grommet

To make the Rope Grommet, use a single strand of natural fiber rope that has been unlayed but retains its spiral shape. Use a length about three and a half times the circumference of the Grommet you want to make.

1 Make a circle out of the center section, and start wrapping one of the ends just as you would start a Multiple Overhand Knot.

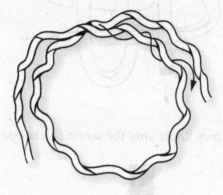

2 Continue these wraps, following the natural spiral shape of the strands, all the way around the circle. At this point, it should look like a ring of three-strand rope with one strand missing.

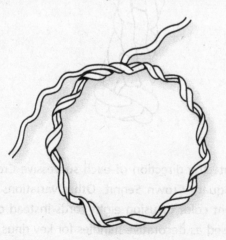

3 Now use other the end to fill in the place of the missing strand. Twisting it slightly as you go may help it seat better. Finish by tying the two ends in a Half Knot, just as you would in the first part of a Reef Knot, and then tuck the ends over and under the strands in the manner of the Back Splice (Chapter 4).

Making Rope Grommets can help you better understand the structure of three-strand rope. Because synthetic rope tends to forget its shape when unlayed, it is awkward to use for making a Grommet.

Coxcombing

The most basic form of Coxcombing is known as French Whipping and is best tied with small string that helps keep a rope end from fraying. For three-strand Coxcombing, follow steps 2 through 4.

 To form French Whipping, make a set of continuous Half Hitches around a bar or rail.

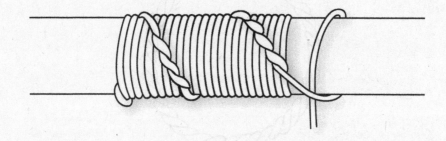

2 Seize three cords to a bar or rail, and start Half Hitches in alternating directions, as shown (see Chapter 12 for details on seizing).

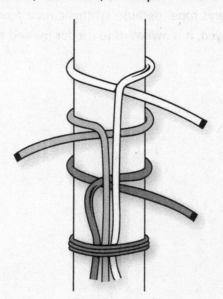

3 Continue by always taking the last cord used and making a Half Hitch in the direction opposite to the previous one.

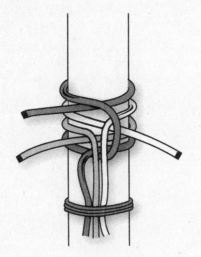

4 Tighten each hitch as you go, and it will form a pattern similar to a Three-Strand Braid along its length.

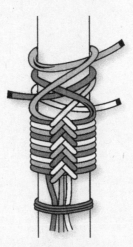

Coxcombings are generally made as protective coverings or over handles or rails to provide a better grip. Other "whippings" to protect rope ends are shown in Chapter 12.

11

Special-Purpose Knots

JUST LIKE TOOLS IN YOUR TOOLBOX, some knots serve a variety of applications, and others tend to be associated with specific tasks. Some activities, like fishing or mountain climbing, have a number of knots associated with them. This chapter is a brief survey of special-purpose knots and the activities that make use of them.

For a Special Purpose

There are numerous reasons why particular knots come to be associated with specific applications or uses. Sometimes the properties of the knots themselves make them favorites for certain applications. The shape of an object that the rope is secured to can result in a particular hitch that will work with that object. Even the cordage material used can affect the choice of knots.

As you can see throughout this book, different knots have distinct properties that make them useful for different tasks. Some knots might be especially secure, while others are good for quick release. Some might be chosen for their ability to be adjusted after tying, while others are preferred because they stay locked. Even the appearance of the finished knot can be important, whether to confirm that it is tied correctly, or just for decoration. As a result, some knots have come to be associated with a particular use just because they are the best choice for the job.

Ⓔ QUESTION?

Is tradition the last word on what is the best knot for a certain application?
Absolutely not. The popular use of some knots can actually be traced back to errors in early knot-tying publications. Sometimes different knots should be used due to a change in the material of the cordage. So, if you are staying up to date on cordage changes in your preferred activity, you should also stay up to date on knots for that activity.

If rope must be secured to an object of a particular shape, not just any hitch will do. One example is the Barrel Sling, shown in Chapter 7. In boating, rope is often tied to a horn cleat, which is illustrated in this chapter along with the hitch that is used with it, called the Cleat Hitch. Tying off to barrels or horn cleats would not work with most hitches, so special hitches have come to be used almost exclusively with them, and have even come to be named after them.

Ⓔ FACT

Using specific knots for specific tasks results in a kind of standardization that can make activities safer and more efficient. When more than one person is involved with rope and knot applications, using different knots for the same job can lead to confusion. If you were crewing on a sailing ship at night during a storm, you certainly wouldn't want the ropes to be secured differently than what you expect.

Size and cordage material can significantly affect the choice of knots used with it. And by extension, activities that use particular types of cordage tend to have many knots that are associated with that activity. For some applications, it is necessary that the cordage floats, be fireproof, small, clear, conduct or not conduct electricity, or have other properties, all of which require different knots. The traditional knots used in many activities have changed over the years to match a change in the cordage used, such as the replacement of natural fiber ropes with more slippery synthetics.

By Activity or Pursuit

Many activities are specialized in both application and in the material of cordage used, which results in a large number of knots being associated with them. Some pursuits, like fishing or mountain climbing, have whole books published just on knots for these fields.

Go Fishing

Fishing is a pursuit that has a particularly rich assortment of knots associated with it. Many of the knots are similar in style because of their suitability for the small and slippery monofilament they are tied in, and many are varied because of the need for different kinds of attachments, that is, terminal tackle. Fishermen often consult fishing-knot books and other publications to learn new fishing knots. It also helps to consult printed materials from the manufacturers of newer fishing lines to get advice on what knots work best with the new lines.

 FACT

Some knots retain their names from the application or profession they were used for, even though that particular use is no longer common. The Packer's Knot was originally a type of Butcher's Knot, even though butchers use tape now. And many knots keep their name from their use on square-rigged sailing vessels, such as the Bowline and the Buntline Hitch.

The nature of nylon monofilament is what determines many of the knots used for fishing. In general, these knots tend to have many turns with the standing part leading straight through the center of the turn before becoming a part of it. When a standing part does this, it is said to have a "good lead." Knots with a good lead will have a higher breaking strength than those without. Knots like the Bowline or the Overhand Knot have lower breaking strengths because monofilament is somewhat self-cutting in knots with few turns. Monofilament is also damaged from friction when the knot is pulled tight, but this is lessened with the use of a lubricant such as water or saliva. Because fishing lines tend to have a specific strength limit, it is important not to weaken the line at the knot.

Ⓔ ESSENTIAL

Many fishing knots need to capsize when tightened to their final form. You can feel the knot doing this as slight pings in the line as you pull it tight. When not fully tightened, you can sometimes hear these pings as the knot finishes capsizing when under the pull of a fish. Because larger lines take more pull to capsize, fewer loops are sometimes used. A knot that needs to be capsized when tightened can easily come untied if it isn't.

Some properties of fishing knots are the result of the small diameter of the line. Many general-purpose knots must be carefully and evenly worked down to their final tightened form to be safe and reliable, but this is difficult with thin fishing line. Fishing knots can be tied with large loops and crossing turns to accommodate large hands, and then pulled down to a small size without being carefully worked into a final shape. Many knots, like the Multiple Overhand Uni-Knots and the Clinch Knot, change shape as they are tightened, which is necessary for them to be strong and secure.

Modern science continues to provide us with new kinds of fishing line, both braided and single strand. For some, you can continue to use fishing knots that are now used on monofilament, and before that, catgut. Some can be better used with different knots, and some people enjoy experimenting with which knots work best with different lines. Some of these new lines are so thin and strong that they can easily cut into your skin when pulling them tight. Gloves can provide some protection.

Rock Climbing and Mountain Rescue

Rock climbing and mountain rescue involves specialized ropes and knots. Controlling your weight suspended from a rope is helped by special hardware used in combination with unique friction hitches. The rope used, called Kernmantle, has a rough outer coating to protect it from abrasion, and special friction knots are chosen that will not damage this outer layer. General knots like those throughout this book are also employed, including some based on the Figure Eight form.

Ⓔ ALERT!

Great care must be taken when using a knot under different circumstances than you would normally use and trust it in. While many loops, bends, and hitches can be used in a wide variety of applications, some knots behave very differently when used with different materials or attachments.

Boating and Sailing

Because boats don't stay where you park them like cars do, they need anchor ropes and dock lines to control them when not under power. Often, these lines need to be fastened to a particular shape, an example of which is the horn cleat. Especially on sailboats, horn cleats are mounted on several places throughout the boat, so knowledge of the Horn Cleat Hitch is important. A fixed loop will fasten to many different shapes, and by converting it to a running loop as shown in Chapter 6, even large posts can be accommodated.

Getting Dressed and the Rest of Daily Life

Tying neckties is also a specialty. Some knots look better than others when tied in the flat material of a necktie. They are generally tied in the form of a hitch or noose, so they can be adjusted in size without leaving slack around the collar. Many necktie knots, described with terms like Four-in-the-Hand, or Windsor, do not work well with rope, but hold their form well with flat material. An Overhand Knot can be used, and a very common necktie knot is made with the Buntline Hitch (described in Chapter 7). In this chapter, you'll learn a modified version of the Buntline Hitch tied with a necktie.

The Buntline Hitch may be a bit conservative for some well-dressed knot tyers, but there are many more variations, suitable for every style and occasion. Your local clothing store may have a free pamphlet with different variations. Very few of them are knots commonly used with cordage. Most necktie knots are used only when tied in a tie, and have no redeeming qualities when tied in rope.

There are numerous other activities that involve specialized knots, and becoming skilled in them is greatly aided by having a skill in general knots. A basic understanding of the differences between bends, loops, and hitches—and knowing a few of each—will help you with a great many applications.

Line to Reel or Spool

Also called the Arbor Knot or Reel Knot, this knot will get you started when winding line onto a spool.

1 Bring the running end around the spool and tie an Overhand Knot around the standing part.

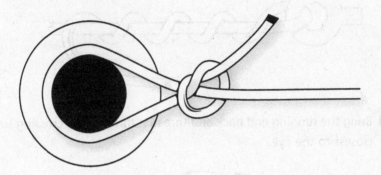

2 Make another Overhand Knot, close to the first, and trim the end short.

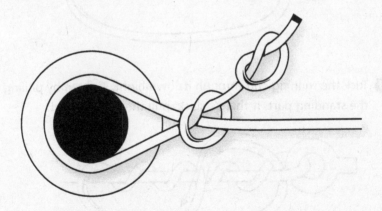

The second Overhand Knot should be tied close to the first, and the very tip should be cut short to avoid tangling with the line as it is wound to the spool. Fingernail clippers make easy work of cutting fishing line close to a knot, but take care not to nick the knot with the clippers.

Improved Clinch Knot

This knot is a useful fishing knot that works well with thin monofilament.

1 Pass the running end through the hook eye or other attachment point, then make three to five wraps around the standing part.

2 Bring the running end back and thread it through the crossing turn closest to the eye.

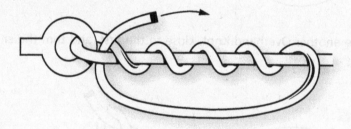

3 Tuck the running end through its own bight. Tighten by pulling on the standing part. If there's slack, pull the running end.

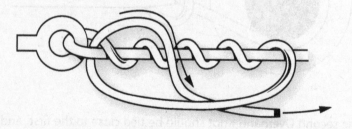

Thin monofilament requires more wraps than thicker line does, and even one wrap can make the difference as to whether it slips under strain. It is difficult to pull this knot down when tied in thick line.

Palomar Hook Knot

Because the Palomar Hook Knot is strong and secure, many recreational and professional fishermen make it their favorite hook tie.

1 Fold the end of the line over and pull the bight through the eye of hook or lure.

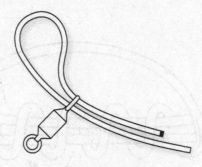

2 Use the bight to tie an Overhand Knot.

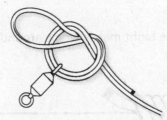

3 Pass the hook or swivel through the bight of the running end. Take out slack with both ends together, and finish tightening with the standing part.

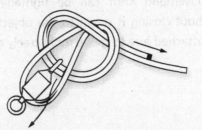

Note that in order to tie the Palomar, the eye should be large enough to pass a bight through it.

Uni-Knot

Also called the Grinner Knot, the Uni-Knot makes for a strong attachment to hooks, lures, or swivels.

1 Pass the running end through the eye, bring it back along the standing part, and form a Multiple Overhand Knot.

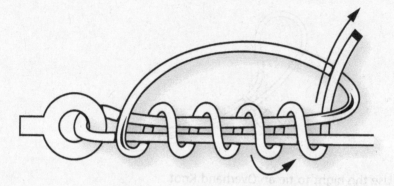

2 Tighten so that the bight makes wraps around the center.

The Multiple Overhand Knot can be tightened down on the standing part, without closing it down to the object to make a loop knot, allowing an attached lure to move more freely and realistically in the water.

Double Uni-Knot

Whereas the Fisherman's Knot and Double Fisherman's Knot (Chapter 5) make a bend by tying an Overhand Knot around each other's standing part, this excellent bend, called the Double Uni-Knot or the Double Grinner Knot, uses four or more Overhand Knots. The Double Uni-Knot is great for joining fishing lines.

 Overlap the ends of two ropes and use one end to tie a multiple Overhand Knot around the standing part of the other line.

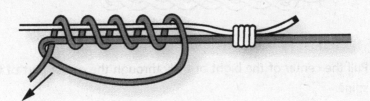

 Tighten down, as shown.

Dropper Loop

Also called the Blood Loop, the Dropper Loop is yet another useful fishing knot based on the series of Overhand Knots.

1 Make a Multiple Overhand Knot with four tucks.

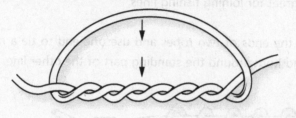

2 Pull the center of the bight or belly through the center part of the spine.

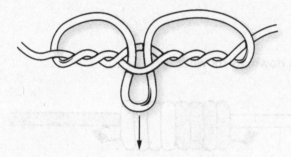

3 Tighten the loop.

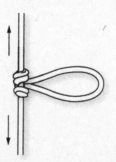

The Dropper Loop can be used to position additional flies, weights, or hooks along a fishing line.

Cleat Hitch

When tied correctly, the Cleat Hitch has a distinctive loop, with one line on top crossing two parallel lines under it.

1 Pass the line once around the base, and bring it diagonally across the top.

2 Pass the running end under one end of the cleat and back diagonally across and on top of the previous pass.

(continued)

Cleat Hitch (continued)

3 Form a crossing turn with the running end on the bottom.

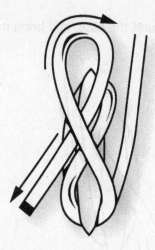

4 Next, drop the crossing turn over the cleat end and pull tight.

5 Or you could finish with a quick-release slipped version.

The most common mistake with this hitch is to make too many wraps and crossings, which can cause it to jam when releasing, making you look like you don't belong near a boat. The Cleat Hitch is not considered a permanent connection but is fairly secure when the rope used is not too big or small for the horn cleat. The slipped version needs a steady load to keep its hold.

Buntline Hitch (Necktie)

A basic way of tying a necktie is by using the Buntline Hitch (illustrated in Chapter 7). First, practice it on a rope. Once you get the hang of it, move on to a necktie.

1 First, practice tying the Buntline Hitch.

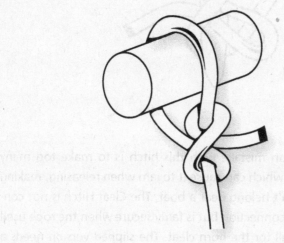

2 Now, do the same with a necktie, using the wide part as the running end.

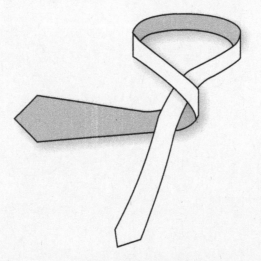

3 Continue, just as in the Buntline Hitch.

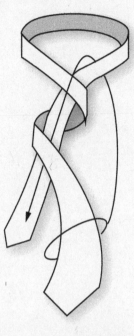

4 Snug down and adjust for neat appearance.

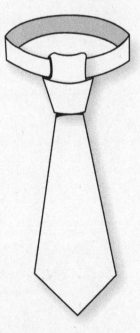

● Continue just as in the Double knot.

● Slide down and adjust for neat appearance.

12

Protecting and Storing Rope

EVERYTHING YOU DO WITH ROPE—from selection and coiling to using it and deciding when to retire it—falls under the category of rope management. This chapter discusses the many skills that are involved with preparing, storing, and caring for rope.

(E) ALERT!

Just as the tools in your workshop or craft closet are easily damaged when used for the wrong application, using the wrong knot can damage rope. The more competent you become at knot tying, the better your cordage will hold up.

Basic Rope Management

Many of the skills you need to care for rope have already been covered throughout this book. The most important rope management skill is simple: using ropes properly. Tying knots that jam can damage the fibers of rope, and even more damage will result from having to pry a jammed knot apart. Tying hitches that are adjustable can aid in keeping slack out of the rope and can help prevent stress damage from shock loading. And, of course, ropes fare much better when they are properly matched to the application.

Many activities that use specific knots and ropes also have their own methods of rope care and management. For example, those who use ropes for climbing or rescue usually take great care not to step on them. Because the rope structure consists of a central core surrounded by a stiff outer layer, this core can take damage from a boot heel that will not be noticeable. Also, fishermen store fishing line away from direct sunlight to protect it from ultraviolet radiation, which might result in premature line weakness.

Much of the rope work methodology we use today was perfected on sailing ships. For centuries, operating a square-rigged sailing vessel required an army of men plying their craft with rope. Because their principal tool for working with rope was the marlinespike, described in Chapter 7, this craft became known as "marlinespike seamanship," and this term is still used today.

Storing Rope in a Coil

Sometimes it is more challenging to store rope than to use it. The best way to store rope is by wrapping the entire length into a coil and tying a part of itself around the coil to keep it secure. When rope turns into a tangle, it's annoying, but what's worse is that it will get twisted, with very sharp turns or kinks. These can damage rope fibers, making it much weaker. Coiling rope is also helpful because rope can be dangerous under foot when loose, especially on boats.

Ⓔ ESSENTIAL

Twists and kinks can get into many of the items we use. They can damage electrical cords and often get in the cord between the phone base and receiver. Sometimes it gets so kinked that it will not extend to its normal length. To get these kinks out, just suspend the earpiece by the cable, and let it spin until the extra twists are out.

Basic Coiling Techniques

You can coil the rope by reaching for each new length with the right hand and adding it to the coil held in the left hand. Stiffer or more tightly laid rope will have more of a tendency to twist into a figure-eight shape than looser rope will. To counteract this tendency, try giving the rope a right-hand twist with each turn of the coil. As you reach out your right hand and grip the rope with your palm away from you, twist your hand and the rope as if you were turning a screwdriver to tighten a screw. Even if you're left-handed, you should still coil them in a clockwise direction because most three-stranded ropes are twisted in a right-handed direction.

If the rope is stiff enough to make even figure eights, then skip the twists and store it as a bundle of that shape. Starting with the first end hanging down lower than the bottom of the coil will help keep it from getting caught in the turns, which can cause the rope to tangle as you uncoil it.

Securing the Coil

As you have seen in many cases throughout this book, you don't always need the end of a rope in order to make a knot. This is also the case when tying the finishing knot on the coils shown in this chapter. It may be that you need to coil up rope that is in service, and the ends are tied to something, as is often the case on a sailboat. In the case of the Gasket Coil, you can start wrapping from the one free end and then make the final knot "in the bight." You can do this with the Figure-of-Eight Coil, also illustrated in this chapter. Many other knots can be made to secure a coil, and people often make up their own way of finishing the coil with the knot of their choice.

Large coils are sometimes bound with several small cords, called "stops," at intervals around the coil. When a rope is stored on a spool, the spool should turn as rope is being taken from it at a 90-degree angle from the turning axis of the spool. If the spool is laid on end with the rope pulled up over one end, each turn will result in a twist in the rope, which can result in kinks. When a coil is bound in the middle as in the case of the Gasket Coil, it is sometimes called a "hank."

 FACT

> Do not confuse the name Figure-of-Eight Coil with a coil that is laid up with figure eights. The Figure-of-Eight Coil has its name because after making a regular circular coil, a knot similar to the Figure Eight Knot is tied at the top around the wraps to keep the coil in place. This is different from the case when each wrap of the coil is laid in the shape of the number eight.

At Rope's Ends

Caring for rope includes taking care of the ends. Ropes are made of many fibers and strands that will separate quickly if not secured. If synthetic three-strand rope is cut without preparation, the three strands will unravel for several feet in just a moment. Other ropes, whether braided or plaited, also unravel or become frayed. The end must be bound in some way, and there are a number of ways to accomplish this.

Tie Up Loose Ends

One way to stop the end of a rope from becoming frayed is to make a binding with string near the end. When this binding consists of many wraps it is called a "whipping," probably named thus because on square-riggers a rope end that was loose would "whip" around in the wind. One way to make this kind of binding is with the Coxcombing (shown in Chapter 10). Two additional methods are illustrated in this chapter. In general, it is best to use natural fiber binding string on natural fiber ropes, and synthetic material on synthetic ropes.

Anything that binds the end of a rope will help stop it from fraying or becoming unraveled, and there are many options. The quickest way is to tie a stopper knot. Even an Overhand Knot will help, although it makes for a bulky solution. For three-strand rope, the Back Splice (Chapter 4) will make a nice-looking end, but it's somewhat bulky as well. If you have string but don't have time to make a proper whipping, a Constrictor Knot makes a good temporary binding.

Use a Lighter

Many people rely on a butane lighter to bind their rope end. Partially melting the rope's end to keep it from fraying is jovially called the Butane Back Splice. After a knot is tied and the running end is cut close, some people like to burn the tip, making it swell in size so that it's less likely to pull back into the knot. When burning the tip, it's important not to let the flame weaken the knot. Stores that sell rope sometimes have a cutting hot wire that leaves the ends heat-sealed after cutting.

However, using a flame only works for synthetic ropes. Heat will not seal the ends of natural fiber ropes because the fibers scorch and burn without melting. Thus, a lighter can also be used to help determine if a rope is natural or synthetic. The only exception to this is Kevlar rope, which scorches without melting.

Ⓔ **FACT**

Using a lighter to seal the ends of a rope can be quick but problematic. Large ropes are difficult to melt evenly, and can result in flaming drips. The ends can also crack or break with use, resulting in an end that can slice through the skin.

Other Methods

Yet another way to bind a rope end is with adhesive tape. When needed, different colors can be used to distinguish different ropes, and the tape can serve as a writing surface for labeling them. Or you can use heat shrink tubing and liquid plastic dip.

When you choose a binding method, keep in mind that some serve an additional purpose. Stiffening the end to aid in threading the rope through a decorative knot, much like the plastic tip on shoelaces, helps to thread the tip through the eyelets set in the shoes.

Seizing

A seizing is similar in form to Square Lashing as shown in Chapter 9, but is for lashing two ropes together. As shown previously, often an extra Half Hitch is put in the running end after tying a knot to help make it secure. For increased security, a seizing can be used to anchor the running end to the standing end. This takes a little extra time but is very secure and can make a knotted attachment a permanent one.

Many people take pride in making a neatly wrapped coil or tying a whipping or seizing just right. The skills of rope management both use and complement many of the other skills of knotting with rope, and the methods that follow will certainly help round out your skills.

 FACT

> To guess by the miles and miles of rope that is used to operate a square-rigged sailing vessel, you would think that a lot of knots are used to secure all that line, but, in fact, the tall masts use many guidelines called "shrouds" that are not tied off with knots but with tackle and seizings. That is one of the reasons that the marlinespike that is used to pull these seizings tight is such an important part of rope management on these vessels.

Figure-of-Eight Coil

Start coiling the rope by folding it in half and making the turns with the doubled line, or by making the turns from one end to the other.

 After wrapping all but the last 2 to 4 feet, depending on the size of the coil, fold a long bight in the end.

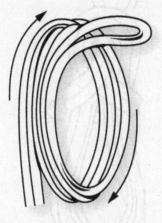

 Pass this bight across the front and around behind the coil.

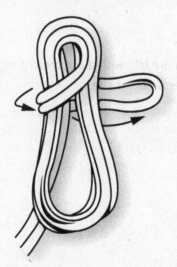

(continued)

Figure-of-Eight Coil (continued)

3 Pass the bight's end over itself and through the coil to the back.

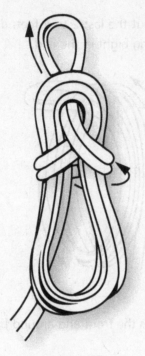

After tying, you are left with a convenient bight that can be used to hang the coil over a nail or peg.

Gasket Coil

Also called the Buntline Coil, the Gasket Coil is often used to tie off excess line on a sailboat. Access to either end is not needed when finishing this coil, which means that the line used in the last tuck can be attached to the rigging.

 After coiling the rope, pass one end several times around the middle of the coil.

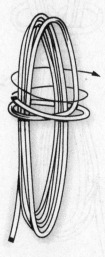

 Pull a bight of the end through the top half of the coil and over the top.

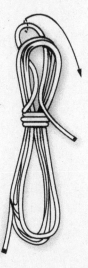

(continued)

Gasket Coil (continued)

3 Pull the bight down to the middle and take out any slack.

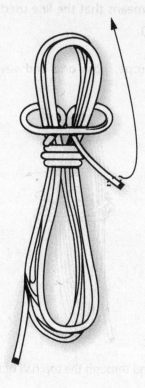

Common Whipping

You can use the following whipping technique to bind a rope's end.

1 Lay a crossing turn along the end of a rope and start making wraps, working inward.

2 Continue making wraps, and tuck the last wrap through the bight. Make sure the wraps are tightly side by side.

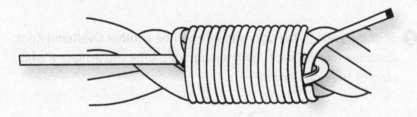

3 Tighten by pulling both ends, so that the crossing stays in the middle of the wraps.

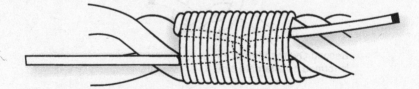

The length of the whipping should be at least as long as the diameter of the rope. If you are tying the whipping over three-strand rope, the direction of the wrapping should be opposite to the direction of the strands. The ends can be trimmed close or knotted together with a Reef Knot.

West Country Whipping

You can make this type of whipping at the end of a rope, or you can add it to a place on the rope where you plan to make the cut, so that you prevent the end from fraying.

1 Tie an Overhand Knot around the rope, leaving both ends of equal length.

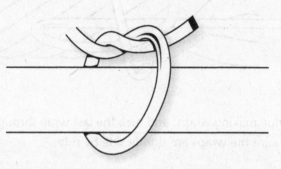

2 Shift the ends to the opposite side and tie another Overhand Knot. Continue making knots, alternating sides, until you achieve a whipping of the right length.

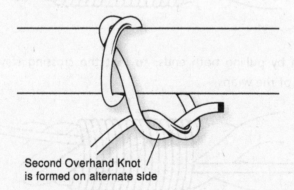

Second Overhand Knot
is formed on alternate side

For variation, start the whipping with a Constrictor Knot and finish with a Reef Knot (see Chapter 8) for added security.

Seizing

For the following method, it's possible to use small string (also used for whipping). The following diagrams show larger rope for purposes of clarity.

 Make a Constrictor Knot around both ropes, leaving one end of the string long enough to make the seizing. Make many wraps for a distance of at least two rope diameters.

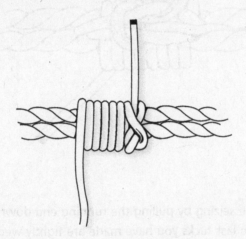

 When the last wrap is made, tuck the string between the ropes and proceed to make exactly two frapping turns.

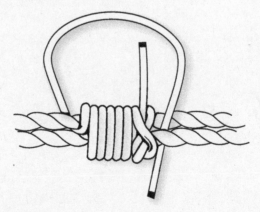

(continued)

Seizing (continued)

3 After exactly two frapping turns, make these tucks and then pull them down between the ropes.

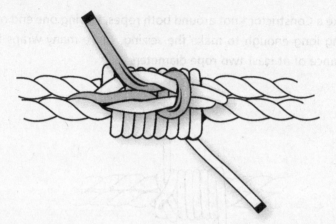

Tighten the seizing by pulling the running end down between the ropes, until the last tucks you have made are tightly wedged between the ropes.

13

Teaching Knot Tying

ONE OF THE MOST REWARDING THINGS about knot tying is teaching it to others. Whether you work with a group of kids or at your local boating club, you'll find yourself having a good time sharing what you know with others and learning more in the process.

Be Prepared

Preparation is important when it comes to teaching anything, and there are a number of ways to prepare for teaching knots. Many of the considerations mentioned in Chapter 3 will aid you here. And, of course, the more practiced you are and the better you know your knotting, the easier it will be to pass on your knowledge and skills to others.

Practice Teaching

Practice tying the knots you will be teaching and watch how you hold the partially completed knots—this step will be an important teaching tool as you show how to tie the knot step by step. You may be so practiced with a particular knot that it is necessary to stop and think about how you tie it.

Also note the look of the knots when they are completed and tightened down correctly. Knowing exactly what the final knot is supposed to look like will help you to judge when your student has tied the knot correctly.

ⒺALERT!

Some knots have more than one way of being tied and some people prefer one method over another, or find one method easier to remember or tie than another. As long as they reach the same end result, their method isn't any less right than yours.

Choose the Right Location

Of course, a good place to teach is important. It should be free of distractions and have adequate space. If you are teaching a class, it will help to know in advance how many students you will have in order to make sure you have the sufficient materials. When you prepare what you will be covering, you may find that it will take more time to cover than you thought. Enlisting the aid of some of the more practiced students can help you to work with more people, checking to see that they are correctly following along with you.

Consider the Presentation

The most common complaint many students in knotting classes have is not being able to see the instructor's work. Some people demonstrate knots with their back to their students and their hands up over their head, so that the students can see from the same perspective as the teacher. Others demonstrate right next to the students—if there are few enough students that all can get a good look.

Don't overlook the value of showing how something can be done wrong. It can be a compelling sight to see a knot that seems secure slip or jam. When showing the Cleat Hitch, show it done incorrectly, with too many wraps and crossovers, and how this compares to being done correctly. If you have extra three-strand synthetic rope to spare, cut it without whipping the end to show how several feet unravel in seconds when the end is not secured.

Invite Guest Speakers

If you are teaching at a place with a repeating venue, like a boating club or scout troop, consider inviting a guest speaker. Many people are glad to talk about their rope usage in their jobs or hobbies. Arborists, boaters, fishermen, rope rescue professionals, even cave divers have interesting things to say about their experiences.

Ⓔ ESSENTIAL

Speakers sometimes have to be encouraged because they may underestimate the value in what they have to share, and you may be surprised at what they recall when you ask them about any exciting or humorous experiences they have had or witnessed.

Use the Right Equipment

For demonstrating knots, try using ropes large enough for people to see. Even fishing knots can be demonstrated with larger rope. Then, when showing tips for how to hold the rope for tying, you can use smaller cordage. It also helps to have ropes of different color—your students will have an easier time distinguishing between two of them.

You might even try those thin, long balloons in different colors—even adults appreciate seeing knots tied with these. They come in diameters as small as 1 inch, and special pumps are available to inflate them.

Since knot tying is learned much better as a hands-on endeavor, you will want to have a variety of ropes and cordage for the students to practice with. You may want to have different sizes for the students to use so that they can practice with a smaller size once they have learned the knot. This is especially true of fishing knots, where nylon fishing line is springy and has to be held differently than other tying materials.

Ⓔ QUESTION?

What is a safe way to cut lengths of rope?
As an alternative to using a knife, surgical scissors are useful for cutting cordage. Tape is a fast way of securing ends from unraveling—a frayed end complicates the learning process of knot tying. For best results, tape the rope first, then cut in the middle of the tape, leaving two taped ends. If you have cut many lengths for the class, you could have the students secure the ends by teaching them how to put on whippings with string.

Here's a list of additional equipment you might need:

- Wooden dowels for practicing hitches and tying lashings
- Horn cleats for teaching boating knots (cheap plastic horn cleats are available from boating stores and are easily attached to a small board for practicing)
- Any other supplies you might need, depending on how the knots you teach will be used

Teaching Knots in Their Context

Learning the proper crossings to form a knot and the proper way to snug it down are very important, but are only part of what should be learned about using knots. Seeing and using knots in the manner that they will be applied is much more helpful in the overall learning process.

There is an endless variety of ways knots can be staged to show them in action. It can be as simple as having someone pull on the standing end of a line to simulate tension as the student is tying it off with a hitch, or as elaborate as assembling a rope bridge with ropes, logs, and lashings.

Ⓔ FACT

While teaching knots in the context in which they will be used, you have the opportunity to demonstrate important safety habits. For example, have someone lightly tug randomly on a rope while someone else is trying to attach it to a horn cleat. This can help the knot tyer learn that a boat being jostled around by waves can pull on the rope, risking fingers becoming caught and injured between the rope and the horn cleat.

Basic Application Ideas

If you are teaching an Anchor Hitch, it helps to include the hardware that you will be knotting to and, if possible, show how a short length of chain fastened between the end of the anchor line and the anchor helps hold the line horizontally from the anchor.

If you are teaching the Tautline Hitch or the Guy Line Hitch, consider using a couple of them to stretch a tarp or side of a tent so that the students can see the effect of adjusting them in combination to achieve the desired results.

When teaching the Trucker's Hitch or the Wagoner's Hitch, tie them as if securing cargo, to show how they fasten and how they release. The Trucker's Hitch should also be demonstrated as pulling tackle, which teaches the concept of leveraged pull. It can be very instructive for a young child to win a game of tug-of-war with a larger child due to the inequity of this arrangement. It should also be pointed out that when the pull is three to one, the distance the parts move is by the opposite ratio.

With Safety in Mind

Sometimes it is difficult to simulate how the knot will be used. Climbing knots should be learned well before trusting your weight to them, so they must be practiced under supervision to make sure they are done correctly. A student who is very confident about his or her abilities will feel differently when about to suspend his or her weight with them from a great height.

Ⓔ ESSENTIAL

Some knots that are relatively new to knotting are quite astounding, and they need to be tinkered with to get a feel for how they work. The Constrictor Knot has an amazing grip, and it is instructive to try it with different ropes around different objects. The Icicle Hitch has to be tried to be believed, and should be tried around even slippery and tapered objects to appreciate its hold.

Loads of Fun Activities

You can make learning knots interesting by associating the process with a particular activity. If you're teaching younger children, this method will help hold their attention for a longer period of time. Games, projects, and even competitions add spice to learning knots. Girl and Boy Scout activities involve knotting in a number of ways, and some examples are mentioned here.

When combined with activities, students can see the knots at work and associate a particular performance with certain knots. Scouts can take part in setting up camp, from rigging lines to keep supplies away from raccoons to mounting tarps and tents. They can see firsthand how the right application of a few knots can turn a few coiled ropes into a base camp.

A fishing trip can begin with a lesson on fishing knots. Then, tying the knots for actual fishing contributes to learning in a number of ways. Repetition is very important for learning knots, and by having to tie them your students will get the benefits of practice right away. Much can be learned about knots and their properties if you see them "in action." Your students will see when some knots slip and evaluate what knots they were, how they were tied or tightened, and what changes might be made to improve performance in the future. The Clinch Knot is an example of a knot where experimentation is important to see how many coils should be used in the knot for it to hold, while also being tightened down without too much pull.

Games and Competitions

Scouting events are known for their schedule of competitions, and these are excellent for learning knots. Based on speed, skill, cooperation, or any combination of these, competition can help learning in many ways.

Ⓔ FACT

Tying a knot one-handed is a very important skill to be taught. A great many activities that require knotting also tend to occupy you with other tasks. Many pursuits require you to hang on to something with one hand, making it very important to be able to tie knots with the other one.

Games based on skill have obvious benefits and can involve demonstration of knot-tying skills and use of judgment. Extra degrees of difficulty can be added, such as trying to tie a knot behind your back, one-handed, or blindfolded. The knot tyers' judgment can be tested by assigning a task to see which knot the contestants will pick to do the job.

Testing Speed

Speed is the basis for many student competitions, as it is easy to explain the rules and judge the winner. A common speed competition popular with scouting and other organizations is based on the time it takes to tie a certain six knots in succession with different ropes for each. The knots are the Square Knot, Sheet Bend, Sheepshank, Clove Hitch, Round Turn and Two Half Hitches, and the Bowline. It takes a bit of practice to do these in less than 20 seconds, and in case you were wondering, the best time measured is 8.1 seconds.

Speed knot tying can involve any combination of knots. For scouting groups, sometimes the Figure Eight and the Tautline Hitch are included and the Sheepshank is left out. When lashing is included in timed games, the goal is usually to complete some lashed structure, sometimes as a team, and then accomplish a task with this structure to illustrate its successful and sturdy completion. This can involve something simple like lashing a tool to the end of a pole for better reach, or something elaborate like lashing together furniture.

Testing Skill

Other competitions can be based on skill. One example is comparing the strength of fishing knots. Since fishing line can come in predetermined line strength of just a few pounds, this can easily be done. Two students can each fasten opposite ends of the same fishing line to a large paper clip or other object. Then, by each pulling on one end in a kind of tug-of-war, the weaker knot will either break or come untied. You might have each person pull on the end that the other tied, so that when the knot gives way, the fishing line will fling back at the one who tied it. And, by the way, you might want a couple of goggles on hand for this. This game of "knot wars" is also handy for comparing the strength of different types of fishing knots.

Knotting Projects

There are many kinds of construction projects that are both fun and educational. The number of crafts that involve knot tying are limitless, and there are countless books and Web sites devoted to this subject. Some projects make objects to decorate scout troop meeting rooms or yacht club lobbies. Even a simple rope mat can add a bit of nautical flair to a room (see Chapter 10).

Some projects—like knot boards—can serve as educational exhibits. A knot board is easily made with a small piece of plywood, a staple gun to fasten completed knots to it, and some labels. A labeled knot board is a common decoration for scout troop meeting places and boating clubs. Some are very elaborately decorated, with braiding for the borders, and maybe a nautical painting featured in the middle.

 FACT

Scout troops on pioneer outings often fashion large structures using lashings as the principal construction method. The Boy Scouts of America publish a pioneering pamphlet that teaches rope skills and ideas for many construction projects, including bridges, towers, ladders, and more.

Making a Grommet, as shown in Chapter 10, is a good small project to help people become familiar with the structure of three-strand rope. Demonstrating rope making is a good activity to do with a group of people because a number of people can be involved at one time. Instructions for rope making can be found in many books as well as online.

The techniques and recommendations in this chapter can be followed closely or can just be used as a guide to lead you to ideas of your own. Teaching knot tying can be a learning experience in itself, and a lot of fun at that. A little extra effort goes a long way, but whatever you do, students will appreciate your efforts and greatly benefit from them.

The Journey Continues

KNOTTING AND ROPE WORK is a much bigger subject than can be covered in one book, and there are many ways to continue and expand your learning. Whether you are pursuing knot tying as a hobby or taking up some activity that makes specialized use of knotting, there is always more to learn. This chapter is a guide to how you can expand your knowledge of knotting.

Learn More in a Particular Area

This book is, for the most part, a general introduction to knots and is not specific to any one activity that requires the use of knots. It is meant to give you the kind of knowledge needed to get the most out of more specialized books when you try to understand them. So, if you take up sailing, fishing, or any other activity, you will be in good shape to learn the knotting that is specific to that activity.

Some activities involve advanced training, where you can learn knots and rope rigging specific to that activity. It may be important to learn the conventions of how rope is used specifically in that pursuit. When teamwork is involved, it may be necessary for more than one person to use rope in the same manner to reduce any confusion that might occur. So even if you know a better way to tie something, it might be safer for you to use rope in a manner expected by the others that may have to work with you.

FACT

Some pursuits have books published about them that are entirely about the knots just for that particular activity. You have probably seen books specializing in fishing knots, but there are also specialty books on sailing knots, climbing knots, magic knots, and many more. These books are not only educational, but can also be a lot of fun, especially if you already have a general understanding of knots.

Beyond These Pages

You might continue your learning of knotting because of a particular activity you are pursuing, or you might want to expand your knowledge of a particular area introduced in this book, like loops or hitches, for instance. This section will help you get the most out of learning from your activities and give you a nearly chapter-by-chapter rundown on how to go further with the concepts introduced in this book.

ESSENTIAL

When the weather is too bad to enjoy a favored outdoor activity, working with the knots used with your pursuit might be an excellent substitute. If it is not a good day for fishing, this may be the ideal time to work on that new fishing knot you've been wanting to try.

The Best Rope for the Job

In Chapter 2, you learned how different ropes have different advantages for a variety of tasks. New ropes are being produced all the time, and whether you are into fishing, mountain climbing, or another activity, you will find that new ropes and twines can offer new possibilities for pursuing your interests. And now that you know a little bit about telling ropes apart, it will help you decide on some purchases the next time you see a mix of them for sale at a flea market or wholesale outlet.

As many ropes as there are available for purchase, it is still an insignificant number compared to the variety of ropes you can make, should you decide to take up the hobby of rope making. The combinations of structures, materials, colors, size, and many other properties are infinite. Winders that do the twisting to make three-strand rope are easy to make or can be purchased. Decorative ropes can be braided in infinite patterns. Raw materials for rope making can be anything from exotic silks to plastic grocery bags. You can even make rope out of toilet paper!

Ⓔ ALERT!

With just a little knowledge about ropes and twine, you may discover the opportunity to find cordage in unlikely places. If you are experimenting with decorative knot tying, for example, discarded window blinds contain very workable and colorful string. Even a lawn mower pull cord might be just the knotting practice cord you have been looking for.

Build on Your Knowledge

Learning knots is something many knot tyers never stop doing. Once you start on your path to learning, you will find out more and more about what works for you. Many people enjoy designing jigs that help hold completed work in place, for everything from fishing knots to elaborate decorative knots. It can be as simple as a small piece of wood with a couple of nails in it, or a large bench with wooden pegs to hold the strands for braiding. You might even want to make apparatus for testing the strength or security of your knots.

Each of the chapters on knots in this book were designed to introduce you to the concepts as well as to the more common knots and structures used for doing that type of knotting. As such, none of the chapters represents the last word on what can be done with these topics. Further research in books or on the Internet will lead you to as many examples as you could ever want.

Stopper Knots

If you are curious about stopper knots, you will find that there are hundreds for you to learn. Just the single-strand knots alone can be tied in limitless ways, and multistrand stopper knots are infinite in the number of decorative variations.

Bends

The same is true for bends—there are whole categories of specialized bends. For example, seizing bends are a category of bends that work best for joining two ropes of very different sizes.

Loops

There's variety in the loop knots as well. The Bowline Loop has become the base for many variations, a number of which were developed to be more secure in synthetic cordage. There is an astounding number of knotting structures that work for loops. You can learn to tie more single loops, nooses, or explore the infinite diversity of multiple loops.

Hitches

Hitches make up the biggest section in many knotting publications. You may want to learn more quick-release hitches, friction hitches, or vibration-proof hitches. Whatever your preference, alternatives abound.

Bindings and Lashings

Any discourse on bindings and lashings can only scratch the surface of the subject, and the chapters in this book are no exception.

For many of the bindings shown here, each represents only one of a whole family of variations. The Packer's Knot is only one of a large family of Butcher's Knots, each with its own different set of properties.

Ⓔ ESSENTIAL

Many of the knots covered in this book are, in fact, only single members of a large family of knots of that type. If you find a particular knot or type of knot that interests you, a little research may lead you to many more knots. For example, say you want a knot that ties over a rail like the Clove Hitch, but acts as a more secure binding. In addition to the Constrictor Knot, there are dozens of knots that fit the bill.

You have certainly noticed that packages and cargo are secured using more than one knot in combination. There are also endless ways of rigging cordage for this job, both in how the ropes are arranged and how they are tied off. Even the number of ways a gift box can be decoratively tied allows you to tie many different gifts without repeating.

A Word on Decoration

Decorative knotting is a large subject by itself, encompassing many styles and crafts. Any decorative knot you see in the chapter on decorative knotting can be explored in nearly infinite variety. The Three-Strand Braid is merely an example of a type of braid that can be tied with any number of strands, and any given number of strands can be combined in numerous patterns. The Ocean Plait Braid is an example of a type of knot that can be used to make mats in a host of patterns in many sizes.

The Turk's Head Knot is very popular among knot-tying hobbyists, who enjoy its many different combinations of leads and bights. Some tyers approach the subject of Turk's Heads with an eye toward the mathematics of which patterns make a symmetrical result, while others delve into the many objects that can be made from them. Even more variations come into play when a pattern other than the over-one-under-one pattern is considered, and more possibilities still when more than one cord is added in, usually of a different color.

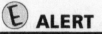

ALERT

For many there is a sense of intimidation at the thought of trying variations of decorative knots. But like regular knotting—and many other pursuits, for that matter—it is what you don't know that seems intimidating. After making just a little progress, whole worlds of possibilities will seem accessible and enjoyable.

Special Concerns

Special knots abound for specialized activities, of which only a glimmer could be covered in any one book. The fishing knots covered in Chapter 11 were chosen based on their relevance to other topics introduced in this book, both in function and structure. There are numerous publications and Web sites dedicated to fishing knots. Moreover, specific varieties of fishing styles have many knots continually being developed for them.

Though the Cleat Hitch is useful to a large number of boaters, there is a wide variety of anchoring hardware for docking, each with different possible knotting styles. References on boating and dock lines also include ways to secure dock lines that account for large tidal ranges, and even storms. You will also find information on using dock lines for controlling boat position while docking and undocking. That is just the subject of docking. Boating references, especially for sailing, have much to teach about knotting and rope work.

Rope Management

The chapter on rope management introduces methods for storing rope, securing the ends to prevent unraveling, and seizing. The two methods for coiling rope presented are both common, but many more are also available (the coiling is usually done the same, the difference being the knot that secures the coil).

The two methods presented for whipping the tips of rope are good techniques for introducing the concept, but there are more as well. Some are more secure, while others can be quite decorative, or both. Some designs are specific to three-strand rope, in that the crossings fit down into the grooves between the strands. Some whippings require a large needle to sew the whipping twine through the center of the rope, a technique that makes it very secure from slipping off the end.

There is not as much variation to seizings. The style introduced in this book is efficient, although some methods secure the ends differently, especially if the seizing is done with doubled twine.

Ⓔ FACT

Many of the skills of rope management are boating-oriented, and many people take pride in it. Good rope management on a boat is considered good seamanship, and you may get judged or find yourself judging others' boating skills by the way they stow their ropes or dock their boat, or whether they do their own splicing. When you have learned the Cleat Hitch correctly, for instance, you may not be able to resist seeing how other boaters have tied off their boats as you walk along a dock.

The Options Are Infinite

You have no doubt come to the conclusion by now that there is no limit to your options for further exploring the subject of knotting. It is most beneficial to learn a wide variety of general concepts, such as hitches and binding knots, even if you plan to specialize in some other area, because knotting structures and techniques overlap the different areas. You will then be better prepared to take advantage of the many different sources of specialty areas. And as shown in the next section, you may find that you can be your own best source of continued learning.

Don't Be Afraid to Experiment

If you want to learn more about knotting, you don't necessarily need to consult other references. You may be amazed at what you can do just by tinkering. There are many ways to discover knotting on your own, and this section will cover many of them, getting you started on a journey that can go as far as you want to take it.

Ⓔ QUESTION?

How much do I need to know about knotting before I start experimenting?
You don't have to be an expert at knotting to experiment. It can be as easy as asking yourself, "What would happen if I changed this?" It's amazing how much can be explored with just a little knowledge, and the wait at the doctor's office will never seem long again.

Try Making Modifications

When even one thing is changed about a knot, it should be considered a completely different knot, with different properties and uses. The change can be as minor as modifying a crossing or making different use of the leads coming from the knot. There are a variety of approaches to trying different knots, and you will no doubt prefer some to others, and may even devise some of your own.

Try combining concepts you already know. Some of the knots in this book show the last tuck with the bight instead of the running end, making it a slipknot. Try this with any knot. Sometimes it will completely release the knot, and sometimes it won't. You could try making more than just the last tuck with a bight, or even the whole knot that way. It's just one simple concept that can give you a world of things to try. You can also try doubling a component, as in making a crossing turn a double crossing turn, making a tuck through a crossing turn twice instead of once. The possibilities are endless.

Tying "In the Bight"

When a knot is tied with the running end, sometimes the same knot can be tied without it. This is what you do when tying a knot "in the bight." An example of this is the Clove Hitch. To test a knot for this possibility, tie it the regular way with the running end, then try to untie it without using the running end. If you can untie a knot without using the running end, then you can tie it without the running end. And if you succeeded in untying it without the running end, just watch how it untied, and you will understand how to tie it.

 FACT

Many times when you are trying a variation, your result will be another common knot, maybe even one described in this book. This is not a failure, and you can use this experience to learn more about the structure of the knot. You may find that you now have a new way of thinking about that knot's form, and you may have even found a new way of tying it.

Learn to Tie by Untying

Perhaps the most powerful tool to give you insight into tying methods for knots is to watch knots as they are untied. No matter how familiar you are with a knot, there are probably more ways to consider its construction than what you already know. After you have tied a knot, many concepts can be learned from watching it in the process of being taken apart. You may see a way to make the knot different, or notice similarities between it and other knots. Perhaps the most productive use of this technique is that you will learn different ways that the knot may be tied.

Ⓔ ESSENTIAL

Another approach to take with trying new knots is changing the tying procedure. Look at the setup in your hands, and maybe twist a loop a different way before completing, or maybe change the order of the tucks. This technique alone can lead in many directions with a wide variety of results.

Start from Scratch

Most of the techniques mentioned so far involve making a knot that you already know, and then changing it. You can also explore from scratch, using a string with no knot or even curve. This can be a lot of fun, and if you like mathematics you can even come up with a number system to keep track of all the combinations you try. However, there are a couple of points you should keep in mind if you do this. One is that modern mathematics is not up to the task of telling even simple knots apart, which means that even though you will find new knots with this method, you will not find all of the possibilities. The second is that you will miss whole categories of useful and decorative knots, working your way through thousands of combinations without some whole categories ever being tried.

One way to use mathematics is to help you keep track of what you have tried. It will also help prevent you from missing a possibility. One example of this is with the Overhand Bends of Chapter 5. The four bends (Ashley's Bend, Hunter's Bend, Zeppelin Bend, and the Butterfly Bend) are all made by interlocking two Overhand Knots. There are actually many more ways to interlock two Overhand Bends. Since there are three internal segments that the running end of another rope can pass through and it may be done from the back or the front, you have six different ways of tying this knot. For this type of bend, the running end will pass through twice, and each Overhand Knot can be left- or right-handed. Assigning a number or letter to each segment can help you keep track of which combinations you have tried.

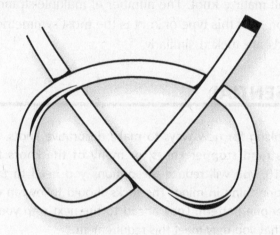

SEGMENTS OF THE OVERHAND KNOT

This is just one example of how you can keep track of what you have and have not tried. Like all experimentation, some will make very good bends, while others will be useless. Until you try it, you won't know what you are going to get.

Build on What You've Learned

You can experiment with any of the knots in this book, using all of the techniques discussed so far. The more solid grasp you have of basic knot structures and the principles of what makes a knot a good one, the more fruitful your experiments will be.

Looking at this book almost chapter by chapter, here are some considerations and ideas of what to look for.

Unlikely materials can make for unique handmade rope. Use red, white, and green strands to make rope for the Christmas holiday season. You can use it as ribbon for presents, or to make decorations.

Single-strand stopper knots can be simple or very involved, and many of them look like buttons. Even an Overhand Knot takes on many different appearances when the running end or a bight is tucked back into one of its segments. Sometimes this method makes a small matlike knot. The number of multiple-strand stopper knots is legion, and this type of knot is the most symmetrical when all the strands are tucked similarly.

(E) ESSENTIAL

When looking for new ways to make decorative knots, such as multistrand stopper knots, or many of the knots from Chapter 10, you will reduce the options you need to try by keeping one thing in mind: The tucks should follow an over-one-under-one pattern. Look ahead to the next step you will need so that you may meet this requirement.

There are lots of ways to make loops, both at the end of a rope and in the bight. Any single-strand stopper knot tied with the end folded over makes a loop knot because the running end makes a loop, and because it is a bight, it doesn't have to be near the end. Multiple loops offer more possibilities, and in some cases, a multiple-loop knot is of the exact same structure as a coil secured with that knot. For example, a coil that is secured at the top with the Bowline is the same as the Portuguese Bowline made with extra loops.

Hitches can be thought of as a slip loop, or as a binding knot with one of the leads acting as a standing part. If it is a complication in rope that attaches it to something, you have a hitch.

Bindings can be changed in all sorts of ways. The crossings of circling knots like the Constrictor Knot can be changed, and different knots for package ties can be combined in many ways. You might even build a Tautline Hitch into a package or bundle tie so that it can be adjusted.

Decorative knots can be changed for different sizes and looks. You can try increasing the number of crossings, doubling or tripling the cords, or even making the cords of different colors. If you get ideas from other references for additional decorative knots, you can still expand on what you find. There is no limit. Some people enjoy the challenge of making decorative knots with especially small or large cordage. Even very involved knots can be made small enough to be earrings. When you are practiced with the Monkey's Fist, you might even try making some small enough for earrings, or large enough for a doorstop. Many knots have an unexpected look when their size is exaggerated or different cordage material is used for them.

(E) ALERT

Learning from other people is an excellent way to increase your knotting skill. Most people will gladly share their knowledge, and may even surprise themselves with how many tricks of the trade they know.

Marlinespike seamanship tends to bring out both the artist and the handyman in boaters. Some like to secure a coil rope with the knot of their own choosing, and show off their favorite method of keeping the end of a rope from fraying. Most decorative forms of Coxcombing also serve well as a rope whipping, so you can just pick the pattern you want the end of your ropes to look like.

A Number of Knots

Beginning knot tyers tend to judge their skill by counting how many knots they know. Hopefully by now you have seen that understanding structures and concepts is more important than numbers. And once you start to learn variations of knots, you may not even be able to count what you know.

Knot Discoveries

Using the techniques in this chapter, and even by accident, you will tie many knots you have never seen before, and probably many that have never appeared in publications. Knotting hobbyists have tied thousands of variations of every category of knots, and some have even published some of their efforts in booklets and journal articles.

Since there is no official registry for knots, official names cannot be bestowed on a particular knot. If you have a great hitch that you want to name after your dog, you are probably out of luck. You can, however, join the International Guild of Knot Tyers, share your explorations with other members at meetings, and even display them. There are many regional branches, and membership is open to anyone interested in knots.

Testing Your Knot

After you learn a knot, you can test your skill with it. The most important test with any knot is to use it in an application. There are many ways that using it for a particular purpose can seem different than when you are practicing with it. By simulating conditions that you may be under when you need to tie your knot, you can test your abilities with it.

Clearly, knot tying is a journey you can take in any number of directions. You can take guides with you, take directions of your own, or both. Whoever said there was "nothing new under the sun" has never played with string, and never caught the perfect fish with a knot of his or her own design.

APPENDIX A

Glossary of Terms

age of sail: The time period before steam engines, when ships large and small used mainly wind for locomotion.

belay: To secure a rope to an anchoring point; in rock climbing, to secure your position.

bend: A knot for joining two ropes together at their ends.

bight: A section of the rope often pulled to a tight curve to become part of a knot.

bind: To seize, lash, or otherwise trap an object and its components.

braid: The interweaving of multiple strands.

cable-laid rope: Three three-strand ropes twisted together to form a larger twisted rope.

capsized knot: A knot that underwent a change of form due to strain, usually when a curved part straightens, causing the shape of other components of the knot to change.

coil: A rope that has been collected into a stack of crossing turns and (usually) secured with a knot, for storage.

cordage: A general term referring to ropes and twines.

coxcombing: A continuous set of hitching of one or more strands to cover an object, usually bar-shaped.

crossing knot: A knot made by one rope around another at the point where it crosses it, then continuing past it.

crossing turn: A circle made of rope where the bases cross each other.

double: To use two cords instead of one, laid parallel to each other.

eye: A closed loop in rope, whether it is spliced, seized, or knotted.

fibers: The smallest threadlike components or cordage.

fid: A cylinder that is tapered to a point at one end, used for separating the lay of twisted rope when splicing.

fixed loop: Also called a "locked loop," a fixed loop is a type of loop knot that does not allow the loop to change size, either by pulling on the standing part or the running end.

frapping turn: A wrap made across the middle of a set of turns already made for a lashing, used to tighten and secure them.

frayed: Unraveled, usually referring to the tip of a rope.

guy lines: Stays, or support lines that help secure tall objects, such as poles.

halyard: Name given to rope on a boat that raises and lowers sails.

hank: A coil of rope that is secured at the middle with a number of wraps.

hawser: Refers to three-strand twisted rope, is a nautical term.

hitch: A knot that fastens a rope to an object.

jam: When a knot cannot be untied readily.

kink: A tight turn in rope that can form when it has extra twists in it due to handling. It is damaging to the rope fibers.

knot: Any complication in rope that has the potential for the rope to act differently than if it were not there. Often refers to a structure that will remain in place under normal use.

lanyard: A strap or short length of rope or braid that serves as a handle. It is generally made into a loop and is often used on tools to prevent their loss.

lariat: Also called a "lasso," it is a rope made into a slip loop, often used like a snare.

lashing: Using multiple wraps and frapping turns to secure two or more poles together.

lead: Refers to the standing and running parts of the rope that exit from a finished knot. Also refers to their direction.

leveraged tie: A fastening or hitch that allows you to apply more tension on an object than you are exerting to tighten it.

line: How rope on a boat is referred to when in use.

loop knot: A knot that locks a section of rope into a circle or other closed form.

marlinespike: Similar to a fid and generally made of metal, it is also used as a grip for pulling twine tightly for seizings.

nautical: Pertaining to the sea or boats.

noose: A slipped loop that is closed by pulling on the standing part.

plait: A form of braid, making a rope of noncircular cross section, or flat braid.

reeve: To pass a rope through the lead of a pulley or other tackle.

riding turns: A second set of turns, usually over a seizing, and having one less turn than the set beneath it.

rope: Cordage that is too large in cross section to be referred to as twine. It is generally made up of more than one strand or component.

round turn: When a rope is wrapped around an object such that it passes behind it twice.

running end: Also called the end, the working end, and the tag end; refers to the tip of the rope when used in forming a knot.

seizing: A form of lashing, used to secure one rope to another, often the running end back to the standing knot, after the knot is formed.

sennit: Braided cordage, also called sinnet.

sheath: The part of a rope that forms its outer covering, when it has a "sheath and core" structure.

shock loading: Placing temporary tension on a slack rope as it comes under sudden strain.

slack: When there is room to pull on a rope or knot, without tighten-ing it.

sling: A ready-made form of rope, usually a closed loop, that can readily be applied to something to serve as a hitch.

slip knot: A knot where the last tuck is made with the running end folded over into a bight, such that it can be released by just pulling on the running end.

slip noose: A knot with a loop that closes down in size by pulling on the standing part; it can usually be completely untied by pulling the standing part all the way through.

snug: To take the slack out of a knot and tighten it.

spill: When a knot capsizes, loosens or unties, either by accident or on purpose.

splice: To fasten a rope to itself or another rope by interweaving the strands.

standing part: Any part of the rope other than the running end that is not being used as a bight; it does not take part in forming the knot, but only takes strain.

stopper knot: Also called a "terminal knot," a type of knot tied at the end of a rope, usually for the purpose of preventing the rope from unreeving from something or to provide a better handhold.

strain: Also called "tension," strain is the result of the rope performing the basic job that it does, transferring force.

strand: A small single cord, or the largest components of a rope.

strength: The amount of strain or tension that a rope can safely handle, or the amount it can take before breaking. When referring to a knot, it is how much that particular knot weakens a particular cordage when tied in it.

stretch: The property of rope to become longer under strain.

tie: To form a knot from cordage, or to fasten cordage to something with a knot.

tied in the bight: Also called "in-the-bight"; refers to forming a knot without access to either end.

turn: When a rope passes once around an object.

whipping: Wrapping a string or twine repeatedly around a rope near the tip, to secure it from fraying.

yarn: Thin twine formed by twisting together a small group of fibers.

APPENDIX B

Additional Resources

Books

Ashley, Clifford W. *The Ashley Book of Knots* (New York: Doubleday, 1993). This large, hardcover book is considered by many knot tyers as the "bible" on the subject.

Budworth, Geoffrey. *The Complete Book of Sailing Knots* (New York: The Lyons Press, 2000).

Budworth, Geoffrey. *The Ultimate Encyclopedia of Knots and Ropework* (London: Lorenz Books, 1999).

Fry, Eric C. *The Complete Book of Knots & Ropework* (Great Britain: David & Charles, 1994).

Graumont, Raoul, and John Hensel. *Encyclopedia of Knots and Fancy Rope Work*. 4th ed. (Centreville, Maryland: Cornell Maritime Press, 1994).

Leeming, Joseph. *Fun with String* (Toronto, Canada: Dover Publications, Inc., 1985).

Marino, Emiliano. *The Sailmaker's Apprentice* (Camden, Maine: International Marine, McGraw-Hill, 1994, 2001).

Merry, Barbara. *The Splicing Handbook*. 2nd ed. (Camden, Maine: International Marine, McGraw-Hill, 2000).

Miles, Roger E. *Symmetric Bends; How to Join Two Lengths of Cord* (Singapore: World Scientific Publishing, Co., 1995).

Newman, Bob, and Tami Knight. *Knots Around the Home* (Birmingham, AL: Menasha Ridge Press, 1997).

Pawson, Des. *The Handbook of Knots* (New York: DK Publishing, Inc., 1998).

Perry, Gordon. *Knots* (London: Barnes & Noble, Inc., 2002).

Smith, Bruce, and Allen Padgett. *On Rope: North American Vertical Rope Techniques* (Huntsville, AL: National Speleological Society, Inc., 1996).

Toss, Brion. *The Complete Rigger's Apprentice* (Camden, Maine: International Marine, McGraw-Hill, 1997).

Organizations

The International Guild of Knot Tyers
✍ *www.igkt.net*

The International Guild of Knot Tyers is an association of people with interests in knots and knotting techniques of all kinds. They have over 1,000 members worldwide from all walks of life, including academics, surgeons, sailors, athletes, scouters, magicians, farmers, miners, and accountants. Membership is open to anyone interested in knotting (whether expert or simply hoping to learn from others). They also publish a quarterly journal called *Knotting Matters*.

International Guild of Knot Tyers—North American Branch
✍ *www.igktnab.org*

This is a sub-branch of the IGKT, formed in the Northeastern United States. They have biannual conventions for knot tyers to share their knowledge and learn from others.

International Guild of Knot Tyers—Pacific Americas Branch
✍ *www.igktpab.org*

This chapter of the IGKT was formed in Southern California in January 1997 to bring a local focus for knotters in the Western United States, Canada, and Alaska.

Web Sites Worth Visiting

Knots on the Web ✍ *www.earlham.edu/~peters/knotlink.htm*
The largest collection of knotting links on the Internet, this site even includes links to activities that use knotting extensively.

Ropers Knots Page ✍ *www.realknots.com*
This site offers another extensive Internet knotting reference source.

Index

OTHER *EVERYTHING*® TITLES
YOU MIGHT ENJOY . . .

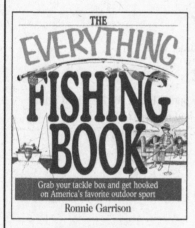

1-58062-865-6
$14.95 (19.95 CAN)

The Everything® Fishing Book is the perfect guide to get you out by your favorite fishing hole, casting your line. The author, experienced fisherman and outdoor sportswriter Ronnie Garrison, provides you with step-by-step instruction on how to choose bait, bait a hook, cast a line, and reel the fish in like a pro. Packed with dozens of clear, easy-to-follow illustrations, this title makes catching the Big One a snap!